SELECTED POEMS

A. B. Paterson

SELECTED POEMS

Angus&Robertson
An imprint of HarperCollins*Publishers*

AN ANGUS & ROBERTSON BOOK
An imprint of HarperCollinsPublishers

First published in Australia in 1992 by
CollinsAngus&Robertson Publishers Pty Limited (ACN 009 913 517)
A division of HarperCollinsPublishers (Australia) Pty Limited
25-31 Ryde Road, Pymble NSW 2073, Australia

HarperCollinsPublishers (New Zealand) Limited
31 View Road, Glenfield, Auckland 10, New Zealand

HarperCollinsPublishers Limited
77-85 Fulham Palace Road, London W6 8JB, United Kingdom

National Library of Australia
Cataloguing-in-Publication data:

Paterson, A.B. (Andrew Barton), 1864-1941

  A.B. Paterson selected poems.

  Includes Index.

  ISBN 0 207 17626 4.

  I. Title

  A821.2

Cover image from the Bulletin 1890, handcoloured by Michèle Lichtenberger
Typeset by Midland Typesetters, Maryborough, Vic.
Printed in Australia by Griffin Paperbacks

5 4 3 2 1
95 94 93 92

CONTENTS

INTRODUCTION

Typically, Australians come to the verse of Banjo Paterson through hearing it recited. My own introduction came from my father reciting 'A Bush Christening' and 'The Man from Ironbark' so far back in my childhood that I have no memory of what age I was. At a party or a dance, in the pub or the club, in an army camp or even during lunch hour at work, someone will start reciting 'Mulga Bill's Bicycle' or 'How the Favourite Beat Us', and people will gather and fall silent to listen. We keep thinking this moment must be obsolete, and disappearing, but it goes on happening. If the mood of the moment is defiant, the choice may be 'How Gilbert Died'. If the mood grows more intransigent, the next item may be by Henry Lawson, pretty well the only other balladist of the 1890s who gets recited now. Often though the mood will turn again, away from the asperities and faded hopes of old politics, back to the timeless headlong idyll of 'The Man from Snowy River' or one of the slower-moving ballads such as 'Clancy of the Overflow' or the 'Travelling Post Office', into which Paterson put a great deal of his yearning for a life he had glimpsed but never followed. In some ways the figure of Clancy, the slow-moving drover, lord of space and the past-become-perpetual, is Paterson's other self, his muse. Clancy is the beckoning figure of Paterson's most meditative moments. When he is close on the track of this keeper of the old Australian ways is usually when he achieves those stretches of timeless presence that make him a poet.

Probably the other main way in which young Australians come to Paterson, though then they may never come any closer or learn his name, is through being obliged to stumble through the modified Cowan version of 'Waltzing Matilda' at some cheery-beery occasion overseas, since for millions beyond our shores and quite a few at home, Matilda is the only Australian song. Nothing much else of Paterson's is sung: that other old, now-faded Australian standard 'The Road to Gundagai' shares its title with a ballad of his but doesn't use his words. Paterson and to a lesser extent Henry Lawson are all that is left of recitation now. Once it was a social accomplishment, as mandatory as cards or dancing, and pretty well indispensable to those who couldn't sing. The Bible and an edition of Paterson were often the only books in poorer country homes but millions who loved Paterson didn't really read him, they conned the lines of his ballads to commit them to memory. And this may still be true today. Yet he isn't what scholars call an oral poet. He learned from those and collected their material for publication in his book *Old Bush Songs*. Once or twice he may even have filched something or so improved it that he felt he could call it his own. A case in point is 'A Bushman's Song', a piece whose flavour is so much more tart and intransigent than Paterson usually displays. That one *has* been sung, as a folksong, and that is probably what it is, at bottom, with Paterson as its arranger. Like Kipling, however, Paterson really came out of the newspapers of his day, out of the style of light verse that existed all over the English-speaking world and flooded into the columns of papers from Jubbulpore to Invercargill. He probably ranks just behind Kipling as the greatest exponent of this kind of verse, a fact evinced not least by the continuing wide acceptance of his work and its ability to step at times across even the grimmest class-barrier of all: that which divides educated Australia from everything rural or pastoral.

This newspaper verse flowed together from many older sources. In part it was the new balladry of classes which had always made up ballads and songs but were now rapidly becoming literate. In part it was the gallows-haunting broadsheet ballad come in off the street where it used to be hawked for a penny. In part it was the amateur versifying of young grammar-school blades carving out names for themselves on the frontiers of the world, and in part it was the overspill of music-hall and parlour song. It arose out of the eighteenth century as the newspapers arose, but its high tide came in the nineteenth. It was thus present in Australia from the beginning of newspapers here. Its earlier efforts were often ponderous, sub-classical and longwinded, and in fact longwindedness was something it never fully overcame, even as it lightened and became racier. Serious poets, who saw poetry as an art, sometimes despised the newspaper market, but often they would contribute their squibs and satires to it, and sometimes their serious compositions got into the papers too. As it developed it came to centre upon the celebration of common life from within that life. Quite unlike modern poetry or poetry of many other eras, it was not written over against common experience or in opposition to it. Its attitudes were the common ones of its time, though it often subtly purified these too, lifting them up into their best and most generous form: Paterson nearly always does this, just as Mark Twain did.

Newspaper verse had a much wider range than the section of it we now term Bush Balladry, but its defining limit was popular appeal; unfamiliar subject matter or thinking had to be presented so as to interest, not snub, the ordinary reader. For a century and more this was the poetry of a mass readership, the only such verse to have enjoyed such readership in the English-speaking world. Literary modernism alienated poetry and that mass readership alike, and the newspapers had all dropped verse publishing by the 1930s or at the very latest the 1940s. Paterson is thus the prime surviving representative of a poetics otherwise completely obsolete in our day, one which has been replaced by popular music. He survives because, unlike most of Lawson's work, Paterson's broke through the concerns and quarrels of his period to a timeless myth.

It was a feature of newspaper verse that authors very often signed their work with a nom-de-plume. This gave respectability a licence to be playful or dangerously frank and spared it from humiliation if its verse didn't catch on. When Andrew Barton Paterson published 'Clancy of the Overflow' in the 1889 Christmas edition of the *Bulletin* he was a 25-year-old solicitor with a respected Sydney firm. Love of the country and its traditions had been instilled in him by spending his childhood on Illalong Station, outside Yass in the classic bushranging country of New South Wales, and then by having to leave. When he went away to live, happily enough, in his Barton grandmother's charming old sandstone house right on the harbour shore at Gladesville, first to attend Sydney Grammar School and then to begin work as an articled law clerk, home became a world visited on holidays. From that to making a personal legend of the bush was no very large step. He was one of that growing host of the country-born who could and did respond when the *Bulletin* in 1880 called on Australians to write about the most distinctively Australian subject, outback life. When Paterson began to do so encouragement was showered on him from the start. The verse of the mysterious 'Banjo' was praised on all sides and many speculated about the identity of its author. Paterson did not satisfy this curiosity until six years later with the publication of his first book *The Man From Snowy River and Other Verses*. Within a year this had sold 10 000 copies, and its total sales eventually exceeded 100 000. In a way it has never stopped selling. Bound up inside innumerable editions of the complete poems, it still flows out the bookshop door today. No Australian poet has sold better and only Henry Lawson and C. J. Dennis, whose best-known work *The Sentimental Bloke* is too lengthy and continuous for recitation, have come near to matching his sales.

Such instant and, as it proved, lifelong success gave Paterson the freedom to travel and soon to escape the office altogether. Even before his first book appeared he had gone off courting to remote Dagworth Station outside Winton, in central Queensland. There a local story, still fresh and perhaps connected with the great shearers' strike of only four years previously, moved him to write the original version of 'Waltzing Matilda', loosely fitted to the tune Craigielea and containing a single mounted police trooper with the cap badge number 123. The version in this book displays the beginnings of that shift towards a threesome of troopers which was fixed for all time when M. and W. Cowan rearranged the words early in this century in order to make a better fit with the music.

By 1900 Paterson was a war correspondent in South Africa and at the end of that year he sailed for China to cover the Boxer Rebellion. Arriving after the fighting had ended, he went on to London then returned to lecture on the Boer War in Australian country towns and in New Zealand. In 1903 he married Alice Walker of Tenterfield in northern New South Wales and became a newspaper editor. In 1908 the Patersons bought Coodra Vale station, on the Upper Murrumbidgee, and farmed there till 1914. When the First World War came they sold their property and went to seek war work in France. They ended up in Egypt, Mrs Paterson working for the Red Cross, her husband holding the rank of major in the Remount Department at Heliopolis Racecourse. Supplying riding stock to the Anzac and British mounted divisions in Palestine, the last great cavalry army in history, was perhaps an appropriate job for a poet whose work is so often a jaunty unsentimental farewell to the long age of the horse. After the war the couple settled back in Sydney, where Paterson died in February 1941.

For this selection of Paterson's work I have drawn on the *Collected Verse* compiled and edited by Frederick Macartney and published in 1921 then expanded in 1986 by the poet's granddaughters. I have also followed the arrangement of that book, which leaves intact the three volumes Paterson published in his lifetime plus a posthumous one compiled from his uncollected pieces. My guidelines have been threefold: I have included all the ballads that appealed to me; plus every ballad I have ever heard anyone recite, and I have added all the shorter pieces which seem to me to be real poems, or at least to contain a fair measure of poetry. This is a side of Paterson which people vaguely acknowledge to be there, but which is often overshadowed by the figure of the horsy storyteller with the absolutely regular rhymes and metres. Poems such as 'The Melting of the Snow' or 'Buffalo Country' may usefully vary this impression, just as they vary the pace of the book. A few of them may even give pause to people who have seen Paterson as a writer of negligible literary quality. I don't claim him as a major poet, but he is a real one. And even at his broadest he carries us into a legendary Australia he did much to create, a country in part bygone, in part fictional, in part still there. Between a quarter and a third of the earth's land surface is, after hunting and gathering, really suitable for no other long-term way of life than the pastoral, so very many features of Paterson's idyll are likely to be long-lived over much of the beautiful but merciless semidesert savanna that is Australia. What maintains the real love which many continue to feel for the Banjo and his work though is probably its presentation of the pastoral spirit at its most generous, its most balanced and its happiest. At times he rivals Lawson in his sharp repudiation of injustice and meanness but this sharpness never becomes dominant. We are more conscious nowadays of how every human spirit has its dark and hidden sides but Paterson rarely stresses these and never lets them defeat us.

LES MURRAY
Bunyah, NSW

Prelude

I have gathered these stories afar,
    In the wind and the rain,
In the land where the cattle camps are,
    On the edge of the plain.
On the overland routes of the West,
    When the watches were long,
I have fashioned in earnest and jest
    These fragments of song.

They are just the rude stories one hears
    In sadness and mirth,
The records of wandering years,
    And scant is their worth.
Though their merits indeed are but slight,
    I shall not repine,
If they give you one moment's delight,
    Old comrades of mine.

The Man from Snowy River

There was movement at the station, for the word had
    passed around
That the colt from old Regret had got away,
And had joined the wild bush horses—he was worth a
    thousand pound,
So all the cracks had gathered to the fray.
All the tried and noted riders from the stations near and far
Had mustered at the homestead overnight,
For the bushmen love hard riding where the wild bush
    horses are,
And the stock horse snuffs the battle with delight.

There was Harrison, who made his pile when Pardon won
    the cup,
The old man with his hair as white as snow;
But few could ride beside him when his blood was fairly
    up—
He could go wherever horse and man could go.
And Clancy of the Overflow came down to lend a hand,
No better horseman ever held the reins;
For never horse could throw him while the saddle girths
    would stand,
He learnt to ride while droving on the plains.

And one was there, a stripling on a small and weedy beast,
He was something like a racehorse undersized,
With a touch of Timor pony—three parts thoroughbred at
    least—
And such as are by mountain horsemen prized.
He was hard and tough and wiry—just the sort that won't
    say die—
There was courage in his quick impatient tread;
And he bore the badge of gameness in his bright and fiery
    eye,
And the proud and lofty carriage of his head.

But still so slight and weedy, one would doubt his power to
    stay,
And the old man said, 'That horse will never do
For a long and tiring gallop—lad, you'd better stop away,
Those hills are far too rough for such as you.'
So he waited sad and wistful—only Clancy stood his
    friend—
'I think we ought to let him come,' he said;
'I warrant he'll be with us when he's wanted at the end,
For both his horse and he are mountain bred.

'He hails from Snowy River, up by Kosciusko's side,
Where the hills are twice as steep and twice as rough,
Where a horse's hoofs strike firelight from the flint stones
    every stride,
The man that holds his own is good enough.
And the Snowy River riders on the mountains make their
    home,
Where the river runs those giant hills between;
I have seen full many horsemen since I first commenced to
    roam,
But nowhere yet such horsemen have I seen.'

So he went—they found the horses by the big mimosa
    clump—
They raced away towards the mountain's brow,
And the old man gave the orders, 'Boys, go at them from the
    jump,
No use to try for fancy riding now.
And, Clancy, you must wheel them, try and wheel them to
    the right.
Ride boldly, lad, and never fear the spills,
For never yet was rider that could keep the mob in sight,
If once they gain the shelter of those hills.'

So Clancy rode to wheel them—he was racing on the wing
Where the best and boldest riders take their place,
And he raced his stockhorse past them, and he made the
    ranges ring

3

With the stockwhip, as he met them face to face.
Then they halted for a moment, while he swung the
    dreaded lash,
But they saw their well-loved mountain full in view,
And they charged beneath the stockwhip with a sharp and
    sudden dash,
And off into the mountain scrub they flew.

Then fast the horsemen followed, where the gorges deep
    and black
Resounded to the thunder of their tread,
And the stockwhips woke the echoes, and they fiercely
    answered back
From cliffs and crags that beetled overhead.
And upward, ever upward, the wild horses held their way,
Where mountain ash and kurrajong grew wide;
And the old man muttered fiercely, 'We may bid the mob
    good day,
No man can hold them down the other side.'

When they reached the mountain's summit, even Clancy
    took a pull,
It well might make the boldest hold their breath,
The wild hop scrub grew thickly, and the hidden ground
    was full
Of wombat holes, and any slip was death.
But the man from Snowy River let the pony have his head,
And he swung his stockwhip round and gave a cheer,
And he raced him down the mountain like a torrent down
    its bed,
While the others stood and watched in very fear.

He sent the flint stones flying, but the pony kept his feet,
He cleared the fallen timber in his stride,
And the man from Snowy River never shifted in his seat—
It was grand to see that mountain horseman ride.
Through the stringybarks and saplings, on the rough and
    broken ground,
Down the hillside at a racing pace he went;

And he never drew the bridle till he landed safe and sound,
At the bottom of that terrible descent.

He was right among the horses as they climbed the further
    hill,
And the watchers on the mountain standing mute,
Saw him ply the stockwhip fiercely, he was right among
    them still,
As he raced across the clearing in pursuit.
Then they lost him for a moment, where two mountain
    gullies met
In the ranges, but a final glimpse reveals
On a dim and distant hillside the wild horses racing yet,
With the man from Snowy River at their heels.

And he ran them single-handed till their sides were white
    with foam.
He followed like a bloodhound on their track,
Till they halted cowed and beaten, then he turned their
    heads for home,
And alone and unassisted brought them back.
But his hardy mountain pony he could scarcely raise a trot,
He was blood from hip to shoulder from the spur;
But his pluck was still undaunted, and his courage fiery hot,
For never yet was mountain horse a cur.

And down by Kosciusko, where the pine-clad ridges raise
Their torn and ragged battlements on high,
Where the air is clear as crystal, and the white stars fairly
    blaze
At midnight in the cold and frosty sky,
And where around The Overflow the reed beds sweep and
    sway
To the breezes, and the rolling plains are wide,
The man from Snowy River is a household word today,
And the stockmen tell the story of his ride.

Clancy of The Overflow

I had written him a letter which I had, for want of better
   Knowledge, sent to where I met him down the Lachlan,
      years ago;
He was shearing when I knew him, so I sent the letter to
      him,
   Just 'on spec', addressed as follows: 'Clancy, of The
   Overflow'.

And an answer came directed in a writing unexpected,
   (And I think the same was written with a thumbnail
      dipped in tar);
'Twas his shearing mate who wrote it, and *verbatim* I will
      quote it:
   'Clancy's gone to Queensland droving, and we don't
   know where he are.'

In my wild erratic fancy visions come to me of Clancy
   Gone a-droving 'down the Cooper' where the Western
      drovers go;
As the stock are slowly stringing, Clancy rides behind them
      singing,
   For the drover's life has pleasures that the townsfolk
   never know.

And the bush hath friends to meet him, and their kindly
      voices greet him
   In the murmur of the breezes and the river on its bars,
And he sees the vision splendid on the sunlit plains
      extended,
   And at night the wondrous glory of the everlasting stars.

I am sitting in my dingy little office, where a stingy
   Ray of sunlight struggles feebly down between the houses
   tall,

And the foetid air and gritty of the dusty, dirty city
  Through the open window floating, spreads its foulness
    over all.

And in place of lowing cattle, I can hear the fiendish rattle
  Of the tramways and the buses making hurry down the
    street,
And the language uninviting of the gutter children fighting
  Comes fitfully and faintly through the ceaseless tramp of
    feet.

And the hurrying people daunt me, and their pallid faces
    haunt me
  As they shoulder one another in their rush and nervous
    haste,
With their eager eyes and greedy, and their stunted forms
    and weedy,
  For townsfolk have no time to grow, they have no time to
    waste.

And I somehow rather fancy that I'd like to change with
    Clancy,
  Like to take a turn at droving where the seasons come
    and go,
While he faced the round eternal of the cashbook and the
    journal—
  But I doubt he'd suit the office, Clancy, of 'The Overflow'.

Conroy's Gap

This was the way of it, don't you know—
   Ryan was 'wanted' for stealing sheep,
And never a trooper, high or low,
   Could find him—catch a weasel asleep!
Till Trooper Scott, from the Stockman's Ford—
   A bushman, too, as I've heard them tell—
Chanced to find him drunk as a lord
   Round at the Shadow of Death Hotel.

D' you know the place? It's a wayside inn,
   A low grog-shanty—a bushman trap,
Hiding away in its shame and sin
   Under the shelter of Conroy's Gap—
Under the shade of that frowning range,
   The roughest crowd that ever drew breath—
Thieves and rowdies, uncouth and strange,
   Were mustered round at the Shadow of Death.

The trooper knew that his man would slide
   Like a dingo pup, if he saw the chance;
And with half a start on the mountain side
   Ryan would lead him a merry dance.
Drunk as he was when the trooper came,
   To him that did not matter a rap—
Drunk or sober, he was the same,
   The boldest rider in Conroy's Gap.

'I want you, Ryan,' the trooper said,
   'And listen to me, if you dare resist,
So help me heaven, I'll shoot you dead!'
   He snapped the steel on his prisoner's wrist,
And Ryan, hearing the handcuffs click,
   Recovered his wits as they turned to go,
For fright will sober a man as quick
   As all the drugs that the doctors know.

There was a girl in that rough bar
    Went by the name of Kate Carew,
Quiet and shy as the bush girls are,
    But ready-witted and plucky, too.
She loved this Ryan, or so they say,
    And passing by, while her eyes were dim
With tears, she said in a careless way,
    'The Swagman's round in the stable, Jim.'

Spoken too low for the trooper's ear,
    Why should she care if he heard or not?
Plenty of swagmen far and near,
    And yet to Ryan it meant a lot.
That was the name of the grandest horse
    In all the district from east to west;
In every show ring, on every course
    They always counted the Swagman best.

He was a wonder, a raking bay—
    One of the grand old Snowdon strain—
One of the sort that could race and stay
    With his mighty limbs and his length of rein.
Born and bred on the mountain side,
    He could race through scrub like a kangaroo,
The girl herself on his back might ride,
    And the Swagman would carry her safely through.

He would travel gaily from daylight's flush
    Till after the stars hung out their lamps,
There was never his like in the open bush,
    And never his match on the cattle camps.
For faster horses might well be found
    On racing tracks, or on plain's extent,
But few, if any, on broken ground
    Could see the way that the Swagman went.

When this girl's father, old Jim Carew,
    Was droving out on the Castlereagh
With Conroy's cattle, a wire came through

9

To say that his wife couldn't live the day.
And he was a hundred miles from home,
    As flies the crow, with never a track,
Through plains as pathless as ocean's foam,
    He mounted straight on the Swagman's back.

He left the camp by the sundown light,
    And the settlers out on the Marthaguy
Awoke and heard, in the dead of night,
    A single horseman hurrying by.
He crossed the Bogan at Dandaloo,
    And many a mile of the silent plain
That lonely rider behind him threw
    Before they settled to sleep again.

He rode all night and he steered his course
    By the shining stars with a bushman's skill,
And every time that he pressed his horse
    The Swagman answered him gamely still.
He neared his home as the east was bright,
    The doctor met him outside the town:
'Carew! How far did you come this night?'
    'A hundred miles since the sun went down.'

And his wife got round, and an oath he passed,
    So long as he or one of his breed
Could raise a coin, though it took their last
    The Swagman never should want a feed.
And Kate Carew, when her father died,
    She kept the horse and she kept him well:
The pride of the district far and wide,
    He lived in style at the bush hotel.

Such was the Swagman; and Ryan knew
    Nothing about could pace the crack;
Little he'd care for the man in blue
    If once he got on the Swagman's back.
But how to do it? A word let fall
    Gave him the hint as the girl passed by;

Nothing but 'Swagman—stable-wall;
    Go to the stable and mind your eye.'

He caught her meaning, and quickly turned
    To the trooper: 'Reckon you'll gain a stripe
By arresting me, and it's easily earned;
    Let's go to the stable and get my pipe,
The Swagman has it.' So off they went,
    And soon as ever they turned their backs
The girl slipped down, on some errand bent
    Behind the stable, and seized an axe.

The trooper stood at the stable door
    While Ryan went in quite cool and slow,
And then (the trick had been played before)
    The girl outside gave the wall a blow.
Three slabs fell out of the stable wall—
    'Twas done 'fore ever the trooper knew—
And Ryan, as soon as he saw them fall,
    Mounted the Swagman and rushed him through.

The trooper heard the hoofbeats ring
    In the stable yard, and he slammed the gate,
But the Swagman rose with a mighty spring
    At the fence, and the trooper fired too late,
As they raced away and his shots flew wide
    And Ryan no longer need care a rap,
For never a horse that was lapped in hide
    Could catch the Swagman in Conroy's Gap.

And that's the story. You want to know
    If Ryan came back to his Kate Carew;
Of course he should have, as stories go,
    But the worst of it is, this story's true:
And in real life it's a certain rule,
    Whatever poets and authors say
Of high-toned robbers and all their school,
    These horse thief fellows aren't built that way.

Come back! Don't hope it—the slinking hound,
　　He sloped across to the Queensland side,
And sold the Swagman for fifty pound,
　　And stole the money, and more beside.
And took to drink, and by some good chance
　　Was killed—thrown out of a stolen trap.
And that was the end of this small romance,
　　The end of the story of Conroy's Gap.

The Geebung Polo Club

It was somewhere up the country, in a land of rock and
   scrub,
That they formed an institution called the Geebung Polo
   Club.
They were long and wiry natives from the rugged
   mountainside,
And the horse was never saddled that the Geebungs
   couldn't ride;
But their style of playing polo was irregular and rash—
They had mighty little science, but a mighty lot of dash:
And they played on mountain ponies that were muscular
   and strong,
Though their coats were quite unpolished, and their manes
   and tails were long.
And they used to train those ponies wheeling cattle in the
   scrub:
They were demons, were the members of the Geebung Polo
   Club.

It was somewhere down the country, in a city's smoke and
   steam,
That a polo club existed, called the Cuff and Collar Team.
As a social institution 'twas a marvellous success,
For the members were distinguished by exclusiveness and
   dress.
They had natty little ponies that were nice, and smooth, and
   sleek,
For their cultivated owners only rode 'em once a week.
So they started up the country in pursuit of sport and fame,
For they meant to show the Geebungs how they ought to
   play the game;
And they took their valets with them—just to give their
   boots a rub
Ere they started operations on the Geebung Polo Club.

Now my readers can imagine how the contest ebbed and
    flowed,
When the Geebung boys got going it was time to clear the
    road;
And the game was so terrific that ere half the time was gone
A spectator's leg was broken—just from merely looking on.
For they waddied one another till the plain was strewn with
    dead,
While the score was kept so even that they neither got
    ahead.
And the Cuff and Collar captain, when he tumbled off to
    die,
Was the last surviving player—so the game was called a tie.

Then the captain of the Geebungs raised him slowly from
    the ground,
Though his wounds were mostly mortal, yet he fiercely
    gazed around;
There was no one to oppose him—all the rest were in a
    trance,
So he scrambled on his pony for his last expiring chance,
For he meant to make an effort to get victory to his side;
So he struck at goal—and missed it—then he tumbled off
    and died.

By the old Campaspe River, where the breezes shake the
    grass,
There's a row of little gravestones that the stockmen never
    pass,
For they bear a crude inscription saying, 'Stranger, drop a
    tear,
For the Cuff and Collar players and the Geebung boys lie
    here.'
And on misty moonlit evenings, while the dingoes howl
    around,
You can see their shadows flitting down that phantom polo
    ground;
You can hear the loud collision as the flying players meet,

And the rattle of the mallets, and the rush of ponies' feet,
Till the terrified spectator rides like blazes to the pub—
He's been haunted by the spectres of the Geebung Polo
    Club.

The Travelling Post Office

The roving breezes come and go, the reed beds sweep and
    sway,
The sleepy river murmurs low, and loiters on its way,
It is the land of lots o' time along the Castlereagh.

The old man's son had left the farm, he found it dull and
    slow,
He drifted to the great North-west where all the rovers go.
'He's gone so long,' the old man said, 'he's dropped right
    out of mind,
But if you'd write a line to him I'd take it very kind;
He's shearing here and fencing there, a kind of waif and
    stray,
He's droving now with Conroy's sheep along the
    Castlereagh.
The sheep are travelling for the grass, and travelling very
    slow;
They may be at Moondooran now, or past the Overflow,
Or tramping down the black soil flats across by Waddiwong,
But all those little country towns would send the letter
    wrong,
The mailman, if he's extra tired, would pass them in his
    sleep,
It's safest to address the note to "Care of Conroy's sheep",
For five and twenty thousand head can scarcely go astray,
You write to "Care of Conroy's sheep along the
    Castlereagh".'

By rock and ridge and riverside the western mail has gone,
Across the great Blue Mountain Range to take that letter on.
A moment on the topmost grade while open fire doors glare,
She pauses like a living thing to breathe the mountain air,
Then launches down the other side across the plains away
To bear that note to 'Conroy's sheep along the Castlereagh'.

And now by coach and mailman's bag it goes from town to
    town,
And Conroy's Gap and Conroy's Creek have marked it
    'further down'.
Beneath a sky of deepest blue where never cloud abides,
A speck upon the waste of plain the lonely mailman rides.
Where fierce hot winds have set the pine and myall boughs
    asweep
He hails the shearers passing by for news of Conroy's sheep.
By big lagoons where wildfowl play and crested pigeons
    flock,
By campfires where the drovers ride around their restless
    stock,
And past the teamster toiling down to fetch the wool away
My letter chases Conroy's sheep along the Castlereagh.

Saltbush Bill

Now this is the law of the Overland that all in the West obey,
A man must cover with travelling sheep a six-mile stage a
    day;
But this is the law which the drovers make, right easily
    understood,
They travel their stage where the grass is bad, but they
    camp where the grass is good;
They camp, and they ravage the squatter's grass till never a
    blade remains,
Then they drift away as the white clouds drift on the edge
    of the saltbush plains,
From camp to camp and from run to run they battle it hand
    to hand,
For a blade of grass and the right to pass on the track of the
    Overland.

For this is the law of the Great Stock Routes, 'tis written in
    white and black—
The man that goes with a travelling mob must keep to a
    half-mile track;
And the drovers keep to a half-mile track on the runs where
    the grass is dead,
But they spread their sheep on a well-grassed run till they
    go with a two-mile spread.
So the squatters hurry the drovers on by dawn till the fall of
    night,
And the squatters' dogs and the drovers' dogs get mixed in
    a deadly fight;
Yet the squatters' men, though they hunt the mob, are
    willing the peace to keep,
For the drovers learn how to use their hands when they go
    with the travelling sheep;
But this is the tale of a Jackaroo that came from a foreign
    strand,
And the fight that he fought with Saltbush Bill, the King of
    the Overland.

Now Saltbush Bill was a drover tough, as ever the country
    knew,
He had fought his way on the Great Stock Routes from the
    sea to the Big Barcoo;
He could tell when he came to a friendly run that gave him
    a chance to spread,
And he knew where the hungry owners were that hurried
    his sheep ahead;
He was drifting down in the Eighty drought with a mob
    that could scarcely creep,
(When the kangaroos by the thousands starve, it is rough on
    the travelling sheep.)
And he camped one night at the crossing place on the edge
    of the Wilga run,
'We must manage a feed for them here,' he said, 'or the half
    of the mob are done!'

So he spread them out when they left the camp wherever
    they liked to go,
Till he grew aware of a Jackaroo with a station hand in tow,
And they set to work on the straggling sheep, and with
    many a stockwhip crack
They forced them in where the grass was dead in the space
    of the half-mile track;
So William prayed that the hand of fate might suddenly
    strike him blue
But he'd get some grass for his starving sheep in the teeth of
    that Jackaroo.
So he turned and he cursed the Jackaroo, he cursed him
    alive or dead,
From the soles of his great unwieldy feet to the crown of his
    ugly head,
With an extra curse on the moke he rode and the cur at his
    heels that ran,
Till the Jackaroo from his horse got down and he went for
    the drover man;
With the station hand for his picker-up, though the sheep
    ran loose the while,

They battled it out on the saltbush plain in the regular prize
  ring style.

Now, the new chum fought for his honour's sake and the
  pride of the English race,
But the drover fought for his daily bread with a smile on his
  bearded face;
So he shifted ground and he sparred for wind and he made
  it a lengthy mill,
And from time to time as his scouts came in they whispered
  to Saltbush Bill—
'We have spread the sheep with a two-mile spread, and the
  grass it is something grand,
You must stick to him, Bill, for another round for the pride
  of the Overland.'

The new chum made it a rushing fight, though never a blow
  got home,
Till the sun rode high in the cloudless sky and glared on the
  brick-red loam,
Till the sheep drew in to the shelter trees and settled them
  down to rest,
Then the drover said he would fight no more and he gave
  his opponent best.
So the new chum rode to the homestead straight and he
  told them a story grand
Of the desperate fight that he fought that day with the King
  of the Overland.
And the tale went home to the public shools of the pluck of
  the English swell,
How the drover fought for his very life, but blood in the end
  must tell.
But the travelling sheep and the Wilga sheep were boxed on
  the Old Man Plain.
'Twas a full week's work ere they drafted out and hunted
  them off again,
With a week's good grass in their wretched hides, with a
  curse and a stockwhip crack,

They hunted them off on the road once more to starve on
  the half-mile track.
And Saltbush Bill, on the Overland, will many a time recite
How the best day's work that ever he did was the day that
  he lost the fight.

A Mountain Station

I bought a run a while ago,
   On country rough and ridgy,
Where wallaroos and wombats grow—
   The Upper Murrumbidgee.
The grass is rather scant, it's true,
   But this a fair exchange is,
The sheep can see a lovely view
   By climbing up the ranges.

And 'She-oak Flat' 's the station's name,
   I'm not surprised at that, sirs:
The oaks were there before I came,
   And I supplied the flat, sirs.
A man would wonder how it's done,
   The stock so soon decreases—
They sometimes tumble off the run
   And break themselves to pieces.

I've tried to make expenses meet
   But wasted all my labours,
The sheep the dingoes didn't eat
   Were stolen by the neighbours.
They stole my pears—my native pears—
   Those thrice-convicted felons,
And ravished from me unawares
   My crop of paddymelons.

And sometimes under sunny skies,
   Without an explanation,
The Murrumbidgee used to rise
   And overflow the station.
But this was caused (as now I know)
   When summer sunshine glowing
Had melted all Kiandra's snow
   And set the river going.

And in the news, perhaps you read:
   'Stock passing. Puckawidgee,
Fat cattle: Seven hundred head
   Swept down the Murrumbidgee;
Their destination's quite obscure,
   But, somehow, there's a notion,
Unless the river falls, they're sure
   To reach the Southern Ocean.'

So after that I'll give it best;
   No more with Fate I'll battle.
I'll let the river take the rest,
   For those were all my cattle.
And with one comprehensive curse
   I close my brief narration,
And advertise it in my verse—
   'For Sale! A Mountain Station'.

The Man Who Was Away

The widow sought the lawyer's room with children three in
    tow,
She told the lawyer man her tale in tones of deepest woe.
She said, 'My husband took a drink for pains in his inside,
And never drew a sober breath from then until he died.

'He never drew a sober breath, he died without a will,
And I must sell the bit of land the childer's mouths to fill.
There's some is grown and gone away, but some is childer
    yet,
And times is very bad indeed—a livin's hard to get.

'There's Min and Sis and little Chris, they stops at home
    with me,
And Sal has married Greenhide Bill that breaks for Bingeree.
And Fred is drovin' Conroy's sheep along the Castlereagh,
And Charley's shearin' down the Bland, and Peter is away.'

The lawyer wrote the details down in ink of legal blue—
'There's Minnie, Susan, Christopher, they stop at home with
    you;
There's Sarah, Frederick and Charles, I'll write to them to-day,
But what about the other one—the one who is away?

'You'll have to furnish his consent to sell the bit of land.'
The widow shuffled in her seat, 'Oh, don't you understand?
I thought a lawyer ought to know—I don't know what to
    say—
You'll have to do without him, boss, for Peter is away.'

But here the little boy spoke up—said he, 'We thought you
    knew;
He's done six months in Goulburn gaol—he's got six more
    to do.'
Thus in one comprehensive flash he made it clear as day,
The mystery of Peter's life—the man who was away.

The Man from Ironbark

It was the man from Ironbark who struck the Sydney town,
He wandered over street and park, he wandered up and
    down.
He loitered here, he loitered there, till he was like to drop,
Until at last in sheer despair he sought a barber's shop.
''Ere! shave my beard and whiskers off, I'll be a man of
    mark,
I'll go and do the Sydney toff up home in Ironbark.'

The barber man was small and flash, as barbers mostly are,
He wore a strike-your-fancy sash, he smoked a huge cigar;
He was a humorist of note and keen at repartee,
He laid the odds and kept a 'tote', whatever that may be,
And when he saw our friend arrive, he whispered, 'Here's a
    lark!
Just watch me catch him all alive, this man from Ironbark.'

There were some gilded youths that sat along the barber's
    wall.
Their eyes were dull, their heads were flat, they had no
    brains at all;
To them the barber passed the wink, his dexter eyelid shut,
'I'll make this bloomin' yokel think his bloomin' throat is
    cut.'
And as he soaped and rubbed it in he made a rude remark:
'I s'pose the flats is pretty green up there in Ironbark.'

A grunt was all reply he got; he shaved the bushman's chin,
Then made the water boiling hot and dipped the razor in.
He raised his hand, his brow grew black, he paused awhile
    to gloat,
Then slashed the red-hot razor-back across his victim's
    throat;
Upon the newly-shaven skin it made a livid mark—
No doubt it fairly took him in—the man from Ironbark.

He fetched a wild up-country yell might wake the dead to
  hear,
And though his throat, he knew full well, was cut from ear
  to ear,
He struggled gamely to his feet, and faced the murd'rous
  foe:
'You've done for me! you dog, I'm beat! one hit before I go!
I only wish I had a knife, you blessed murdering shark!
But you'll remember all your life the man from Ironbark.'

He lifted up his hairy paw, with one tremendous clout
He landed on the barber's jaw, and knocked the barber out.
He set to work with nail and tooth, he made the place a
  wreck;
He grabbed the nearest gilded youth, and tried to break his
  neck.
And all the while his throat he held to save his vital spark,
And 'Murder! Bloody murder!' yelled the man from
  Ironbark.

A peelerman who heard the din came in to see the show;
He tried to run the bushman in, but he refused to go.
And when at last the barber spoke, and said ' 'Twas all in
  fun—
'Twas just a little harmless joke, a trifle overdone.'
'A joke!' he cried, 'By George, that's fine; a lively sort of lark;
I'd like to catch that murdering swine some night in
  Ironbark.'

And now while round the shearing floor the list'ning
  shearers gape,
He tells the story o'er and o'er, and brags of his escape.
'Them barber chaps what keeps a tote, By George, I've had
  enough,
One tried to cut my bloomin' throat, but thank the Lord it's
  tough.'
And whether he's believed or no, there's one thing to
  remark,
That flowing beards are all the go way up in Ironbark.

On Kiley's Run

The roving breezes come and go
    On Kiley's Run,
The sleepy river murmurs low,
And far away one dimly sees
Beyond the stretch of forest trees—
Beyond the foothills dusk and dun—
The ranges sleeping in the sun
    On Kiley's Run.

'Tis many years since first I came
    To Kiley's Run,
More years than I would care to name
Since I, a stripling, used to ride
For miles and miles at Kiley's side,
The while in stirring tones he told
The stories of the days of old
    On Kiley's Run.

I see the old bush homestead now
    On Kiley's Run,
Just nestled down beneath the brow
Of one small ridge above the sweep
Of river flat, where willows weep
And jasmine flowers and roses bloom,
The air was laden with perfume
    On Kiley's Run.

We lived the good old station life
    On Kiley's Run,
With little thought of care or strife.
Old Kiley seldom used to roam,
He liked to make the Run his home,
The swagman never turned away
With empty hand at close of day
    From Kiley's Run.

We kept a racehorse now and then
    On Kiley's Run,
And neighb'ring stations brought their men
To meetings where the sport was free,
And dainty ladies came to see
Their champions ride; with laugh and song
The old house rang the whole night long
    On Kiley's Run.

The station hands were friends I wot
    On Kiley's Run,
A reckless, merry-hearted lot—
All splendid riders, and they knew
The 'boss' was kindness through and through.
Old Kiley always stood their friend,
And so they served him to the end
    On Kiley's Run.

But droughts and losses came apace
    To Kiley's Run,
Till ruin stared him in the face;
He toiled and toiled while lived the light,
He dreamed of overdrafts at night:
At length, because he could not pay,
His bankers took the stock away
    From Kiley's Run.

Old Kiley stood and saw them go
    From Kiley's Run.
The well-bred cattle marching slow;
His stockmen, mates for many a day,
They wrung his hand and went away.
Too old to make another start,
Old Kiley died—of broken heart,
    On Kiley's Run.

The owner lives in England now
    Of Kiley's Run.
He knows a racehorse from a cow;
But that is all he knows of stock:
His chiefest care is how to dock
Expenses, and he sends from town
To cut the shearers' wages down
    On Kiley's Run.

There are no neighbours anywhere
    Near Kiley's Run.
The hospitable homes are bare,
The gardens gone; for no pretence
Must hinder cutting down expense:
The homestead that we held so dear
Contains a half-paid overseer
    On Kiley's Run.

All life and sport and hope have died
    On Kiley's Run.
No longer there the stockmen ride;
For sour-faced boundary riders creep
On mongrel horses after sheep,
Through ranges where, at racing speed,
Old Kiley used to 'wheel the lead'
    On Kiley's Run.

There runs a lane for thirty miles
    Through Kiley's Run.
On either side the herbage smiles,
But wretched trav'lling sheep must pass
Without a drink or blade of grass
Thro' that long lane of death and shame:
The weary drovers curse the name
    Of Kiley's Run.

The name itself is changed of late
    Of Kiley's Run.
They call it 'Chandos Park Estate'.
The lonely swagman through the dark
Must hump his swag past Chandos Park.
The name is English, don't you see,
The old name sweeter sounds to me
    Of 'Kiley's Run'.

I cannot guess what fate will bring
    To Kiley's Run—
For chances come and changes ring—
I scarcely think 'twill always be
Locked up to suit an absentee;
And if he lets it out in farms
His tenants soon will carry arms
    On Kiley's Run.

In The Droving Days

'Only a pound,' said the auctioneer,
'Only a pound; and I'm standing here
Selling this animal, gain or loss.
Only a pound for the drover's horse;
One of the sort that was ne'er afraid,
One of the boys of the Old Brigade;
Thoroughly honest and game, I'll swear,
Only a little the worse for wear;
Plenty as bad to be seen in town,
Give me a bid and I'll knock him down;
Sold as he stands, and without recourse,
Give me a bid for the drover's horse.'

Loitering there in an aimless way
Somehow I noticed the poor old grey,
Weary and battered and screwed, of course,
Yet when I noticed the old grey horse,
The rough bush saddle, and single rein
Of the bridle laid on his tangled mane,
Straightway the crowd and the auctioneer
Seemed on a sudden to disappear,
Melted away in a kind of haze,
For my heart went back to the droving days.

Back to the road, and I crossed again
Over the miles of the saltbush plain—
The shining plain that is said to be
The dried-up bed of an inland sea,
Where the air so dry and so clear and bright
Refracts the sun with a wondrous light,
And out in the dim horizon makes
The deep blue gleam of the phantom lakes.

At dawn of day we would feel the breeze
That stirred the boughs of the sleeping trees,
And brought a breath of the fragrance rare

That comes and goes in that scented air;
For the trees and grass and the shrubs contain
A dry sweet scent on the saltbush plain.
For those that love it and understand,
The saltbush plain is a wonderland.
A wondrous country, where nature's ways
Were revealed to me in the droving days.

We saw the fleet wild horses pass,
And the kangaroos through the Mitchell grass,
The emu ran with her frightened brood
All unmolested and unpursued.
But there rose a shout and a wild hubbub
When the dingo raced for his native scrub,
And he paid right dear for his stolen meals
With the drovers' dogs at his wretched heels.
For we ran him down at a rattling pace,
While the pack horse joined in the stirring chase.
And a wild halloo at the kill we'd raise—
We were light of heart in the droving days.

'Twas a drover's horse, and my hand again
Made a move to close on a fancied rein.
For I felt the swing and the easy stride
Of the grand old horse that I used to ride
In drought or plenty, in good or ill,
That same old steed was my comrade still;
The old grey horse with his honest ways
Was a mate to me in the droving days.

When we kept our watch in the cold and damp,
If the cattle broke from the sleeping camp,
Over the flats and across the plain,
With my head bent down on his waving mane,
Through the boughs above and the stumps below
On the darkest night I would let him go
At a racing speed; he would choose his course,
And my life was safe with the old grey horse.
But man and horse had a favourite job,

When an outlaw broke from a station mob,
With a right good will was the stockwhip plied,
As the old horse raced at the straggler's side,
And the greenhide whip such a weal would raise,
We could use the whip in the droving days.

'Only a pound!' and was this the end—
Only a pound for the drover's friend.
The drover's friend that had seen his day,
And now was worthless, and cast away
With a broken knee and a broken heart
To be flogged and starved in a hawker's cart.
Well, I made a bid for a sense of shame
And the memories dear of the good old game.

'Thank you? Guinea! and cheap at that!
Against you there in the curly hat!
Only a guinea, and one more chance,
Down he goes if there's no advance,
Third, and the last time, one! two! three!'
And the old grey horse was knocked down to me.
And now he's wandering, fat and sleek,
On the lucerne flats by the Homestead Creek;
I dare not ride him for fear he'd fall,
But he does a journey to beat them all,
For though he scarcely a trot can raise,
He can take me back to the droving days.

Lost

'He ought to be home,' said the old man, 'without there's
    something amiss.
He only went to the Two-mile—he ought to be back by this.
He *would* ride the Reckless filly, he *would* have his wilful
    way;
And, here, he's not back at sundown—and what will his
    mother say?

'He was always his mother's idol, since ever his father died;
And there isn't a horse on the station that he isn't game to
    ride.
But that Reckless mare is vicious, and if once she gets away
He hasn't got strength to hold her—and what will his
    mother say?'

The old man walked to the sliprail, and peered up the
    dark'ning track,
And looked and longed for the rider that would never more
    come back;
And the mother came and clutched him, with sudden,
    spasmodic fright:
'What has become of my Willie? Why isn't he home
    tonight?'

Away in the gloomy ranges, at the foot of an ironbark,
The bonnie, winsome laddie was lying stiff and stark;
For the Reckless mare had smashed him against a leaning
    limb,
And his comely face was battered, and his merry eyes were
    dim.

And the thoroughbred chestnut filly, the saddle beneath her
    flanks,
Was away like fire through the ranges to join the wild mob's
    ranks;

And a broken-hearted woman and an old man worn and
    grey
Were seaching all night in the ranges till the sunrise brought
    the day.

And the mother kept feebly calling, with a hope that would
    not die,
'Willie! where are you, Willie?' But how can the dead reply;
And hope died out with the daylight, and the darkness
    brought despair,
God pity the stricken mother, and answer the widow's
    prayer!

Though far and wide they sought him, they found not
    where he fell;
For the ranges held him precious, and guarded their
    treasure well.
The wattle blooms above him, and the bluebells blow close
    by,
And the brown bees buzz the secret, and the wild birds sing
    reply.

But the mother pined and faded, and cried, and took no rest,
And rode each day to the ranges on her hopeless, weary
    quest.
Seeking her loved one ever, she faded and pined away,
But with strength of her great affection she still sought
    every day.

'I know that sooner or later I shall find my boy,' she said.
But she came not home one evening, and they found her
    lying dead,
And stamped on the poor pale features, as the spirit
    homeward pass'd,
Was an angel smile of gladness—she had found the boy at
    last.

Over the Range

Little bush maiden, wondering-eyed,
   Playing alone in the creek bed dry,
In the small green flat on every side
   Walled in by the Moonbi Ranges high;
Tell us the tale of your lonely life,
   'Mid the great grey forests that know no change.
'I never have left my home,' she said,
   'I have never been over the Moonbi Range.'

'Father and mother are both long dead,
   And I live with granny in yon wee place.'
'Where are your father and mother?' we said.
   She puzzled awhile with thoughtful face,
Then a light came into the shy brown eye,
   And she smiled, for she thought the question strange
On a thing so certain—'When people die
   They go to the country over the range.'

'And what is this country like, my lass?'
   'There are blossoming trees and pretty flowers,
And shining creeks where the golden grass
   Is fresh and sweet from the summer showers.
They never need work, nor want, nor weep;
   No troubles can come their hearts to estrange.
Some summer night I shall fall asleep,
   And wake in the country over the range.'

Child, you are wise in your simple trust,
   For the wisest man knows no more than you.
Ashes to ashes, and dust to dust:
   Our views by a range are bounded too;
But we know that God hath this gift in store,
   That when we come to the final change,
We shall meet with our loved ones gone before
   To the beautiful country over the range.

The Boss of the 'Admiral Lynch'

Did you ever hear tell of Chile? I was readin' the other day
Of President Balmaceda and of how he was sent away.
It seems that he didn't suit 'em—they thought that they'd
    like a change,
So they started an insurrection and chased him across the
    range.
They seem to be restless people—and, judging by what you
    hear,
They raise up these revolutions 'bout two or three times a
    year;
And the man that goes out of office, he goes for the
    boundary *quick*,
For there isn't no vote by ballot—it's bullets that does the
    trick.
And it ain't like a real battle, where the prisoners' lives are
    spared,
And they fight till there's one side beaten and then there's a
    truce declared,
And the man that has got the licking goes down like a
    blooming lord
To hand in his resignation and give up his blooming sword,
And the other man bows and takes it, and everything's all
    polite—
This wasn't that kind of a picnic, this wasn't that sort of a
    fight.
For the pris'ners they took—they shot 'em; no odds were
    they small or great,
If they'd collared old Balmaceda, they reckoned to shoot
    him straight.
A lot of bloodthirsty devils they were—but there ain't a doubt
They must have been real plucked 'uns—the way that they
    fought it out,
And the king of 'em all, I reckon, the man that could stand a
    pinch,
Was the boss of a one-horse gunboat. They called her the
    Admiral Lynch.

Well, he was for Balmaceda, and after the war was done,
And Balmaceda was beaten and his troops had been forced
    to run,
The other man fetched his army and proceeded to do things
    brown,
He marched 'em into the fortress and took command of the
    town.
Cannon and guns and horses troopin' along the road,
Rumblin' over the bridges, and never a foeman showed
Till they came in sight of the harbour, and the very first
    thing they see
Was this mite of a one-horse gunboat a-lying against the
    quay,
And there as they watched they noticed a flutter of crimson
    rag,
And under their eyes he hoisted old Balmaceda's flag.
Well, I tell you it fairly knocked 'em—it just took away their
    breath,
For he must ha' known if they caught him, 'twas nothin' but
    sudden death.
An' he'd got no fire in his furnace, no chance to put out to
    sea,
So he stood by his gun and waited with his vessel against
    the quay.
Well, they sent him a civil message to say that the war was
    done,
And most of his side were corpses, and all that were left had
    run;
And blood had been spilt sufficient, so they gave him a
    chance to decide
If he'd haul down his bit of bunting and come on the
    winning side.
He listened and heard their message, and answered them all
    polite,
That he was a Spanish hidalgo, and the men of his race *must*
    fight!
A gunboat against an army, and with never a chance to run,
And them with their hundred cannon and him with a single
    gun:

The odds were a trifle heavy—but he wasn't the sort to
	flinch,
So he opened fire on the army, did the boss of the *Admiral
	Lynch*.
They pounded his boat to pieces, they silenced his single
	gun,
And captured the whole consignment, for none of 'em cared
	to run;
And it don't say whether they shot him—it don't even give
	his name—
But whatever they did I'll wager that he went to his
	graveyard game.
I tell you those old hidalgos so stately and so polite,
They turn out the real Maginnis when it comes to an uphill
	fight.
There was General Alcantara, who died in the heaviest
	brunt,
And General Alzereca was killed in the battle's front;
But the king of 'em all, I reckon—the man that could stand a
	pinch—
Was the man who attacked the army with the gunboat
	Admiral Lynch.

A Bushman's Song

I'm travellin' down to Castlereagh, and I'm a station hand,
I'm handy with the ropin' pole, I'm handy with the brand,
And I can ride a rowdy colt, or swing the axe all day,
But there's no demand for a station hand along the
    Castlereagh.

So it's shift, boys, shift, for there isn't the slightest doubt
That we've got to make a shift to the stations further out;
With the packhorse runnin' after, for he follows like a dog,
We must strike across the country at the old jig-jog.

This old black horse I'm riding—if you'll notice what's his
    brand,
He wears the crooked R, you see—none better in the land.
He takes a lot of beatin', and the other day we tried,
For a bit of a joke, with a racing bloke, for twenty pounds
    a side.

It was shift, boys, shift, for there wasn't the slightest doubt,
That I had to make him shift, for the money was nearly out;
But he cantered home a winner, with the other one at the
    flog—
He's a red-hot sort of pick up with his old jig-jog.

I asked a cove for shearin' once along the Marthaguy:
'We shear non-union, here,' says he. 'I call it scab,' says I.
I looked along the shearin' floor before I turned to go—
There were eight or ten dashed Chinamen a-shearin' in a
    row.

It was shift, boys, shift, for there wasn't the slightest doubt
It was time to make a shift with the leprosy about.
So I saddled up my horses, and I whistled to my dog,
And I left his scabby station at the old jig-jog.

I went to Illawarra where my brother's got a farm,
He has to ask his landlord's leave before he lifts his arm;
The landlord owns the countryside—man, woman, dog, and
    cat,
They haven't the cheek to dare to speak without they touch
    their hat.

It was shift, boys, shift, for there wasn't the slightest doubt
Their little landlord god and I would soon have fallen out;
Was I to touch my hat to him?—was I his bloomin' dog?
So I makes for up the country at the old jig-jog.

But it's time that I was movin', I've a mighty way to go
Till I drink artesian water from a thousand feet below;
Till I meet the overlanders with the cattle comin' down,
And I'll work a while till I make a pile, then have a spree in
    town.

So, it's shift, boys, shift, for there isn't the slightest doubt
We've got to make a shift to the stations further out;
The packhorse runs behind us, for he follows like a dog,
And we cross a lot of country at the old jig-jog.

How Gilbert Died

There's never a stone at the sleeper's head,
    There's never a fence beside,
And the wandering stock on the grave may tread
    Unnoticed and undenied,
But the smallest child on the Watershed
    Can tell you how Gilbert died.

For he rode at dusk, with his comrade Dunn
    To the hut at the Stockman's Ford,
In the waning light of the sinking sun
    They peered with a fierce accord.
They were outlaws both—and on each man's head
    Was a thousand pounds reward.

They had taken toll of the country round,
    And the troopers came behind
With a black that tracked like a human hound
    In the scrub and the ranges blind:
He could run the trail where a white man's eye
    No sign of a track could find.

He had hunted them out of the One Tree Hill
    And over the Old Man Plain,
But they wheeled their tracks with a wild beast's skill,
    And they made for the range again.
Then away to the hut where their grandsire dwelt,
    They rode with a loosened rein.

And their grandsire gave them a greeting bold:
    'Come in and rest in peace,
No safer place does the country hold—
    With the night pursuit must cease,
And we'll drink success to the roving boys,
    And to hell with the black police.'

But they went to death when they entered there,
   In the hut at the Stockman's Ford,
For their grandsire's words were as false as fair—
   They were doomed to the hangman's cord.
He had sold them both to the black police
   For the sake of the big reward.

In the depth of night there are forms that glide
   As stealthy as serpents creep,
And around the hut where the outlaws hide
   They plant in the shadows deep,
And they wait till the first faint flush of dawn
   Shall waken their pray from sleep.

But Gilbert wakes while the night is dark—
   A restless sleeper, aye,
He has heard the sound of a sheepdog's bark,
   And his horse's warning neigh,
And he says to his mate, 'There are hawks abroad,
   And it's time that we went away.'

Their rifles stood at the stretcher head,
   Their bridles lay to hand,
They wakened the old man out of his bed,
   When they heard the sharp command:
'In the name of the Queen lay down your arms,
   Now, Dunn and Gilbert, stand!'

Then Gilbert reached for his rifle true
   That close at his hand he kept,
He pointed it straight at the voice and drew,
   But never a flash outleapt,
For the water ran from the rifle breach—
   It was drenched while the outlaws slept.

Then he dropped the piece with a bitter oath,
   And he turned to his comrade Dunn:

'We are sold,' he said, 'we are dead men both,
    But there may be a chance for one;
I'll stop and I'll fight with the pistol here,
    You take to your heels and run.'

So Dunn crept out on his hands and knees
    In the dim, half-dawning light,
And he made his way to a patch of trees,
    And vanished among the night,
And the trackers hunted his tracks all day,
    But they never could trace his flight.

But Gilbert walked from the open door
    In a confident style and rash;
He heard at his side the rifles roar,
    And he heard the bullets crash.
But he laughed as he lifted his pistol-hand,
    And he fired at the rifle flash.

Then out of the shadows the troopers aimed
    At his voice and the pistol sound,
With the rifle flashes the darkness flamed,
    He staggered and spun around,
And they riddled his body with rifle balls
    As it lay on the blood-soaked ground.

There's never a stone at the sleeper's head
    There's never a fence beside,
And the wandering stock on the grave may tread
    Unnoticed and undenied,
But the smallest child on the Watershed
    Can tell you how Gilbert died.

Shearing at Castlereagh

The bell is set aringing, and the engine gives a toot,
There's five and thirty shearers here are shearing for the
    loot,
So stir yourselves, you penners-up and shove the sheep
    along,
The musterers are fetching them a hundred thousand
    strong,
And make your collie dogs speak up—what would the
    buyers say
In London if the wool was late this year from Castlereagh?

The man that 'rung' the Tubbo shed is not the ringer here,
That stripling from the Cooma side can teach him how to
    shear.
They trim away the ragged locks, and rip the cutter goes,
And leaves a track of snowy fleece from brisket to the nose;
It's lovely how they peel it off with never stop nor stay,
They're racing for the ringer's place this year at Castlereagh.

The man that keeps the cutters sharp is growling in his cage,
He's always in a hurry and he's always in a rage—
'You clumsy-fisted muttonheads, you'd turn a fellow sick,
You pass yourselves as shearers? You were born to swing a
    pick!
Another broken cutter here, that's two you've broke today,
It's awful how such crawlers come to shear at Castlereagh.'

The youngsters picking up the fleece enjoy the merry din,
They throw the classer up the fleece, he throws it to the bin;
The pressers standing by the rack are waiting for the wool,
There's room for just a couple more, the press is nearly full;
Now jump upon the lever, lads, and heave and heave away,
Another bale of golden fleece is branded 'Castlereagh'.

In Defence of the Bush

So you're back from up the country, Mister Lawson, where
    you went,
And you're cursing all the business in a bitter discontent;
Well, we grieve to disappoint you, and it makes us sad to
    hear
That it wasn't cool and shady—and there wasn't plenty
    beer,
And the loony bullock snorted when you first came into
    view;
Well, you know it's not so often that he sees a swell like you;
And the roads were hot and dusty, and the plains were
    burnt and brown,
And no doubt you're better suited drinking lemon squash in
    town.

Yet, perchance, if you should journey down the very track
    you went
In a month or two at furthest you would wonder what it
    meant,
Where the sunbaked earth was gasping like a creature in its
    pain
You would find the grasses waving like a field of summer
    grain,
And the miles of thirsty gutters blocked with sand and
    choked with mud,
You would find them mighty rivers with a turbid, sweeping
    flood;
For the rain and drought and sunshine make no changes in
    the street,
In the sullen line of buildings and the ceaseless tramp of
    feet;
But the bush hath moods and changes, as the seasons rise
    and fall,
And the men who know the bush land—they are loyal
    through it all.

But you found the bush was dismal and a land of no delight,
Did you chance to hear a chorus in the shearers' huts at
     night?
Did they 'rise up, William Riley' by the camp-fire's cheery
     blaze?
Did they rise him as we rose him in the good old droving
     days?
And the women of the homesteads and the men you
     chanced to meet—
Were their faces sour and saddened like the 'faces in the
     street',
And the 'shy selector children'—were they better now or
     worse
Than the little city urchins who would greet you with a
     curse?
Is not such a life much better than the squalid street and
     square
Where the fallen women flaunt it in the fierce electric glare,
Where the sempstress plies her sewing till her eyes are sore
     and red
In a filthy, dirty attic toiling on for daily bread?
Did you hear no sweeter voices in the music of the bush
Than the roar of trams and buses, and the war whoop of
     'the push'?
Did the magpies rouse your slumbers with their carol sweet
     and strange?
Did you hear the silver chiming of the bellbirds on the range?
But, perchance, the wild birds' music by your senses was
     despised,
For you say you'll stay in townships till the bush is civilised.
Would you make it a tea garden and on Sundays have a
     band
Where the 'blokes' might take their 'donahs', with a 'public'
     close at hand?
You had better stick to Sydney and make merry with the
     'push',
For the bush will never suit you, and you'll never suit the
     bush.

A Bush Christening

On the outer Barcoo where the churches are few,
 And men of religion are scanty,
On a road never cross'd 'cept by folk that are lost,
 One Michael Magee had a shanty.

Now this Mike was the dad of a ten-year-old lad,
 Plump, healthy, and stoutly conditioned;
He was strong as the best, but poor Mike had no rest
 For the youngster had never been christened.

And his wife used to cry, 'If the darlin' should die
 Saint Peter would not recognise him.'
But by luck he survived till a preacher arrived,
 Who agreed straightaway to baptise him.

Now the artful young rogue, while they held their collogue,
 With his ears to the keyhole was listenin',
And he muttered in fright while his features turned white,
 'What the divil and all is this christenin'?'

He was none of your dolts, he had seen them brand colts,
 And it seemed to his small understanding,
If the man in the frock made him one of the flock,
 It must mean something very like branding.

So away with a rush he set off for the bush,
 While the tears in his eyelids they glistened—
' 'Tis outrageous,' says he, 'to brand youngsters like me,
 I'll be dashed if I'll stop to be christened!'

Like a young native dog he ran into a log,
 And his father with language uncivil,
Never heeding the 'praste' cried aloud in his haste,
 'Come out and be christened, you divil!'

But he lay there as snug as a bug in a rug,
  And his parents in vain might reprove him,
Till his reverence spoke (he was fond of a joke)
  'I've a notion,' says he, 'that'll move him.'

'Poke a stick up the log, give the spalpeen a prog;
  Poke him aisy—don't hurt him or maim him,
'Tis not long that he'll stand, I've the water at hand,
  As he rushes out this end I'll name him.

'Here he comes, and for shame! ye've forgotten the name—
  Is it Patsy or Michael or Dinnis?'
Here the youngster ran out, and the priest gave a shout—
  Take your chance, anyhow, wid "Maginnis"!'

As the howling young cub ran away to the scrub
  Where he knew that pursuit would be risky,
The priest, as he fled, flung a flask at his head
  That was labelled 'Maginnis's Whisky!'

And Maginnis Magee has been made a J.P.,
  And the one thing he hates more than sin is
To be asked by the folk who have heard of the joke,
  How he came to be christened 'Maginnis'!

How the Favourite Beat Us

'Aye,' said the boozer, 'I tell you it's true, sir,
    I once was a punter with plenty of pelf,
But gone is my glory, I'll tell you the story
    How I stiffened my horse and got stiffened myself.

' 'Twas a mare called the Cracker, I came down to back her,
    But found she was favourite all of a rush,
The folk just did pour on to lay six to four on,
    And several bookies were killed in the crush.

'It seems Old Tomato was stiff, though a starter;
    They reckoned him fit for the Caulfield to keep.
The Bloke and the Donah were scratched by their owner,
    He only was offered three-fourths of the sweep.

'We knew Salamander was slow as a gander,
    The mare could have beat him the length of the straight,
And old Manumission was out of condition,
    And most of the others were running off weight.

'No doubt someone "blew it", for everyone knew it,
    The bets were all gone, and I muttered in spite,
"If I can't get a copper, by Jingo, I'll stop her,
    Let the public fall in, it will serve the brutes right."

'I said to the jockey, "Now, listen, my cocky,
    You watch as you're cantering down by the stand,
I'll wait where that toff is and give you the office,
    You're only to win if I lift up my hand."

'I then tried to back her—"What price is the Cracker?"
    "Our books are all full, sir," each bookie did swear:
My mind, then, I made up, my fortune I played up
    I bet every shilling against my own mare.

'I strolled to the gateway, the mare in the straight way
  Was shifting and dancing, and pawing the ground,
The boy saw me enter and wheeled for his canter,
  When a darned great mosquito came buzzing around.

'They breed 'em at Hexham, it's risky to vex 'em,
  They suck a man dry at a sitting, no doubt,
But just as the mare passed, he fluttered my hair past,
  I lifted my hand, and I flattened him out.

'I was stunned when they started, the mare simply darted
  Away to the front when the flag was let fall,
For none there could match her, and none tried to catch her—
  She finished a furlong in front of them all.

'You bet that I went for the boy, whom I sent for
  The moment he weighed and came out of the stand—
"Who paid you to win it? Come, own up this minute."
  "Lord love yer,' said he, "why, you lifted your hand."

' 'Twas true, by St Peter, that cursed "muskeeter"
  Had broke me so broke that I hadn't a brown,
And you'll find the best course is when dealing with horses
  To win when you're able, and *keep your hands down*.'

Come-by-Chance

As I pondered very weary o'er a volume long and dreary—
For the plot was void of interest—'twas that Postal Guide, in
  fact,
There I learnt the true location, distance, size, and
  population
Of each township, town, and village in the radius of the Act.

And I learnt that Puckawidgee stands beside the
  Murrumbidgee,
And that Booleroi and Bumble get their letters twice a year,
Also that the post inspector, when he visited Collector,
Closed the office up instanter, and re-opened Dungalear.

But my languid mood forsook me, when I found a name that
  took me,
Quite by chance I came across it—'Come-by-Chance' was
  what I read;
No location was assigned it, not a thing to help one find it,
Just an 'N' which stood for northward, and the rest was all
  unsaid.

I shall leave my home, and forthward wander stoutly to the
  northward
Till I come by chance across it, and I'll straightway settle
  down,
For there can't be any hurry, nor the slightest cause for
  worry
Where the telegraph don't reach you nor the railways run to
  town.

And one's letters and exchanges come by chance across the
  ranges,
Where a wiry young Australian leads a pack horse once a
  week,

And the good news grows by keeping, and you're spared
the pain of weeping
Over bad news when the mailman drops the letters in the
creek.

But I fear, and more's the pity, that there's really no such
city,
For there's not a man can find it of the shrewdest folk I
know,
'Come-by-Chance', be sure it never means a land of fierce
endeavour,
It is just the careless country where the dreamers only go.

Though we work and toil and hustle in our life of haste and
bustle,
All that makes our life worth living comes unstriven for and
free;
Man may weary and importune, but the fickle goddess
Fortune
Deals him out his pain or pleasure careless what his worth
may be.

All the happy times entrancing, days of sport and nights of
dancing,
Moonlit rides and stolen kisses, pouting lips and loving
glance:
When you think of these be certain you have looked behind
the curtain,
You have had the luck to linger just a while in
'Come-by-Chance'.

Jim Carew

Born of a thoroughbred English race,
  Well-proportioned and closely knit,
Neat of figure and handsome face,
  Always ready and always fit,
Hard and wiry of limb and thew,
That was the ne'er-do-well Jim Carew.

One of the sons of the good old land—
  Many a year since his like was known;
Never a game but he took command,
  Never a sport but he held his own;
Gained at his college a triple blue—
Good as they make them was Jim Carew.

Came to grief—was it card or horse?
  Nobody asked and nobody cared;
Ship him away to the bush of course,
  Ne'er-do-well fellows are easily spared;
Only of women a tolerable few
Sorrowed at parting with Jim Carew.

Gentleman Jim on the cattle camp,
  Sitting his horse with an easy grace;
But the reckless living has left its stamp
  In the deep drawn lines of that handsome face,
And a harder look in those eyes of blue:
Prompt at a quarrel is Jim Carew.

Billy the Lasher was out for gore—
  Twelve-stone navvy with chest of hair,
When he opened out with a hungry roar,
  On a ten-stone man it was hardly fair;
But his wife was wise if his face she knew
By the time you were done with him, Jim Carew.

Gentleman Jim in the stockman's hut
  Works with them, toils with them, side by side;
As to his past—well, his lips are shut.
  'Gentleman once,' say his mates with pride;
And the wildest cornstalk can ne'er outdo
In feats of recklessness, Jim Carew.

What should he live for? A dull despair!
  Drink is his master and drags him down,
Water of Lethe that drowns all care.
  Gentleman Jim has a lot to drown,
And he reigns as king with a drunken crew,
Sinking to misery, Jim Carew.

Such is the end of the ne'er-do-well—
  Jimmy the Boozer, all down at heel;
But he straightens up when he's asked to tell
  His name and race, and a flash of steel
Still lightens up in those eyes of blue—
'I am, or—no, I *was*—Jim Carew.'

Rio Grande's Last Race

Now this was what Macpherson told
    While waiting in the stand;
A reckless rider, over-bold,
The only man with hands to hold
    The rushing Rio Grande.

He said, 'This day I bid goodbye
    To bit and bridle rein,
To ditches deep and fences high,
For I have dreamed a dream, and I
    Shall never ride again.

'I dreamed last night I rode this race
    That I to-day must ride,
And cant'ring down to take my place
I saw full many an old friend's face
    Come stealing to my side.

'Dead men on horses long since dead,
    They clustered on the track;
The champions of the days long fled,
They moved around with noiseless tread—
    Bay, chestnut, brown, and black.

'And one man on a big grey steed
    Rode up and waved his hand;
Said he, "We help a friend in need,
And we have come to give a lead
    To you and Rio Grande.

'"For you must give the field the slip,
    So never draw the rein,
But keep him moving with the whip,
And if he falter—set your lip
    And rouse him up again.

'"But when you reach the big stone wall,
   Put down your bridle hand
And let him sail—he cannot fall—
But don't you interfere at all;
   You trust old Rio Grande."

'We started, and in front we showed,
   The big horse running free:
Right fearlessly and game he strode,
And by my side those dead men rode
   Whom no one else could see.

'As silently as flies a bird,
   They rode on either hand;
At every fence I plainly heard
The phantom leader give the word,
   "Make room for Rio Grande!"

'I spurred him on to get the lead,
   I chanced full many a fall;
But swifter still each phantom steed
Kept with me, and at racing speed
   We reached the big stone wall.

'And there the phantoms on each side
   Drew in and blocked his leap;
"Make room! make room!" I loudly cried,
But right in front they seemd to ride—
   I cursed them in my sleep.

'He never flinched, he faced it game,
   He struck it with his chest,
And every stone burst out in flame,
And Rio Grande and I became
   As phantoms with the rest.

'And then I woke, and for a space
   All nerveless did I seem;

For I have ridden many a race,
But never one at such a pace
   As in that fearful dream.

'And I am sure as man can be
   That out upon the track,
Those phantoms that men cannot see
Are waiting now to ride with me,
   And I shall not come back.

'For I must ride the dead men's race,
   And follow their command;
'Twere worse than death, the foul disgrace
If I should fear to take my place
   Today on Rio Grande.'

He mounted, and a jest he threw,
   With never sign of gloom;
But all who heard the story knew
That Jack Macpherson, brave and true,
   Was going to his doom.

They started, and the big black steed
   Came flashing past the stand;
All single-handed in the lead
He strode along at racing speed,
   The mighty Rio Grande.

But on his ribs the whalebone stung,
   A madness it did seem!
And soon it rose on every tongue
That Jack Macpherson rode among
   The creatures of his dream.

He looked to left and looked to right,
   As though men rode beside;
And Rio Grande, with foam-flecks white,
Raced at his jumps in headlong flight
   And cleared them in his stride.

But when they reached the big stone wall,
    Down went the bridle hand,
And loud we heard Macpherson call,
'Make room, or half the field will fall!
    Make room for Rio Grande!'

'He's down! he's down!' And horse and man
    Lay quiet side by side!
No need the pallid face to scan,
We knew with Rio Grande he ran
    The race the dead men ride.

By the Grey Gulf-water

Far to the Northward there lies a land,
   A wonderful land that the winds blow over,
And none may fathom nor understand
   The charm it holds for the restless rover;
A great grey chaos—a land half made,
   Where endless space is and no life stirreth;
And the soul of a man will recoil afraid
   From the sphinx-like visage that Nature weareth.
But old Dame Nature, though scornful, craves
   Her dole of death and her share of slaughter;
Many indeed are the nameless graves
   Where her victims sleep by the Grey Gulf-water.

Slowly and slowly those grey streams glide,
   Drifting along with a languid motion,
Lapping the reed beds on either side,
   Wending their way to the Northern Ocean.
Grey are the plains where the emus pass
   Silent and slow, with their staid demeanour;
Over the dead men's graves the grass
   Maybe is waving a trifle greener.
Down in the world where men toil and spin
   Dame Nature smiles as man's hand has taught her;
Only the dead men her smiles can win
   In the great lone land by the Grey Gulf-water.

For the strength of man is an insect's strength,
   In the face of that mighty plain and river,
And the life of a man is a moment's length
   To the life of the stream that will run for ever.
And so it cometh they take no part
   In small-world worries; each hardy rover
Rideth abroad and is light of heart,
   With the plains around and the blue sky over.

And up in the heavens the brown lark sings
   The songs that the strange wild land has taught her;
Full of thanksgiving her sweet song rings—
   And I wish I were back by the Grey Gulf-water.

With the Cattle

The drought is down on field and flock,
   The river bed is dry;
And we must shift the starving stock
   Before the cattle die.
We muster up with weary hearts
   At breaking of the day,
And turn our heads to foreign parts,
   To take the stock away.
      And it's hunt 'em up and dog 'em,
      And it's get the whip and flog 'em,
For it's weary work is droving when they're
        dying every day;
      By stock routes bare and eaten,
      On dusty roads and beaten,
With half a chance to save their lives we
        take the stock away.

We cannot use the whip for shame
   On beasts that crawl along;
We have to drop the weak and lame,
   And try to save the strong;
The wrath of God is on the track,
   The drought fiend holds his sway,
With blows and cries and stockwhip crack
   We take the stock away.
      As they fall we leave them lying,
      With the crows to watch them dying,
Grim sextons of the Overland that fasten
        on their prey;
      By the fiery dust storm drifting,
      And the mocking mirage shifting,
In heat and drought and hopeless pain we
        take the stock away.

In dull despair the days go by
   With never hope of change,

But every stage we draw more nigh
    Towards the mountain range;
And some may live to climb the pass,
    And reach the great plateau,
And revel in the mountain grass,
    By streamlets fed with snow.
        As the mountain wind is blowing
        It starts the cattle lowing,
And calling to each other down the dusty
        long array;
        And there speaks a grizzled drover:
        'Well, thank God, the worst is over,
The creatures smell the mountain grass that's
        twenty miles away.'

They press towards the mountain grass,
    They look with eager eyes
Along the rugged stony pass,
    That slopes towards the skies;
Their feet may bleed from rocks and stones,
    But though the blood-drop starts,
They struggle on with stifled groans,
    For hope is in their hearts.
        And the cattle that are leading,
        Though their feet are worn and bleeding,
Are breaking to a kind of run—pull up,
        and let them go!
        For the mountain wind is blowing,
        And the mountain grass is growing,
They settle down by running streams ice-cold
        with melted snow.

The days are done of heat and drought
    Upon the stricken plain;
The wind has shifted right about,
    And brought the welcome rain;
The river runs with sullen roar,
    All flecked with yellow foam,

And we must take the road once more,
　　To bring the cattle home.
　　　　And it's 'Lads! we'll raise a chorus,
　　　　There's a pleasant trip before us.'
And the horses bound beneath us as we start
　　　　them down the track;
　　　　And the drovers canter, singing,
　　　　Through the sweet green grasses springing,
Towards the far-off mountain land, to bring
　　　　the cattle back.

Are these the beasts we brought away
　　That move so lively now?
They scatter off like flying spray
　　Across the mountain's brow;
And dashing down the rugged range
　　We hear the stockwhip crack,
Good faith, it is a welcome change
　　To bring such cattle back.
　　　　And it's 'Steady down the lead there!'
　　　　And it's 'Let 'em stop and feed there!'
For they're wild as mountain eagles and
　　　　their sides are all afoam;
　　　　But they're settling down already,
　　　　And they'll travel nice and steady,
With cheery call and jest and song we fetch
　　　　the cattle home.

We have to watch them close at night
　　For fear they'll make a rush,
And break away in headlong flight
　　Across the open bush;
And by the campfire's cheery blaze,
　　With mellow voice and strong,
We hear the lonely watchman raise
　　The Overlander's song:
　　　　'Oh! it's when we're done with roving,
　　　　With the camping and the droving,

It's homeward down the Bland we'll go,
  and never more we'll roam';
    While the stars shine out above us,
    Like the eyes of those who love us—
The eyes of those who watch and wait to greet
    the cattle home.

The plains are all awave with grass,
  The skies are deepest blue;
And leisurely the cattle pass
  And feed the long day through;
But when we sight the station gate,
  We make the stockwhips crack,
A welcome sound to those who wait
  To greet the cattle back:
    And through the twilight falling
    We hear their voices calling,
As the cattle splash across the ford and
    churn it into foam;
    And the children run to meet us,
    And our wives and sweethearts greet us,
Their heroes from the Overland who brought
    the cattle home.

Mulga Bill's Bicycle

'Twas Mulga Bill, from Eaglehawk, that caught the cycling
   craze;
He turned away the good old horse that served him many
   days;
He dressed himself in cycling clothes, resplendent to be
   seen;
He hurried off to town and bought a shining new machine;
And as he wheeled it through the door, with air of lordly
   pride,
The grinning shop assistant said, 'Excuse me, can you ride?'

'See here, young man,' said Mulga Bill, 'From Walgett to the
   sea,
From Conroy's Gap to Castlereagh, there's none can ride
   like me.
I'm good all round at everything, as everybody knows,
Although I'm not the one to talk—I *hate* a man that blows.
But riding is my special gift, my chiefest, sole delight;
Just ask a wild duck can it swim, a wildcat can it fight.
There's nothing clothed in hair or hide, or built of flesh or
   steel,
There's nothing walks or jumps, or runs, on axle, hoof, or
   wheel,
But what I'll sit, while hide will hold and girth and straps
   are tight:
I'll ride this here two-wheeled concern right straight away
   at sight.'

'Twas Mulga Bill, from Eaglehawk, that sought his own
   abode,
That perched above the Dead Man's Creek, beside the
   mountain road.
He turned the cycle down the hill and mounted for the fray,
But ere he'd gone a dozen yards it bolted clean away.

It left the track, and through the trees, just like a silver
    streak,
It whistled down the awful slope towards the Dead Man's
    Creek.

It shaved a stump by half an inch, it dodged a big white
    box:
The very wallaroos in fright went scrambling up the rocks,
The wombats hiding in their caves dug deeper
    underground,
As Mulga Bill, as white as chalk, sat tight to every bound.
It struck a stone and gave a spring that cleared a fallen tree,
It raced beside a precipice as close as close could be;
And then as Mulga Bill let out one last despairing shriek
It made a leap of twenty feet into the Dead Man's Creek.

'Twas Mulga Bill, from Eaglehawk, that slowly swam ashore:
He said, 'I've had some narrer shaves and lively rides before;
I've rode a wild bull round a yard to win a five-pound bet,
But this was the most awful ride that I've encountered yet.
I'll give that two-wheeled outlaw best; it's shaken all my
    nerve
To feel it whistle through the air and plunge and buck and
    swerve.
It's safe at rest in Dead Man's Creek, we'll leave it lying still;
A horse's back is good enough henceforth for Mulga Bill.'

The Pearl Diver

Kanzo Makame, the diver, sturdy and small Japanee,
Seeker of pearls and of pearl shell down in the depths of the
   sea,
Trudged o'er the bed of the ocean, searching industriously.

Over the pearl grounds, the lugger drifted—a little white
   speck:
Joe Nagasaki, the 'tender', holding the life line on deck,
Talked through the rope to the diver, knew when to drift or
   to check.

Kanzo was king of his lugger, master and diver in one,
Diving wherever it pleased him, taking instructions from
   none;
Hither and thither he wandered, steering by stars and by
   sun.

Fearless he was beyond credence, looking at death eye to
   eye:
This was his formula always, 'All man go dead by and by—
S'pose time come no can help it—s'pose time no come, then
   no die.'

Dived in the depths of the Darnleys, down twenty fathom
   and five;
Down where by law and by reason, men are forbidden to
   dive;
Down to a pressure so awful that only the strongest survive:

Sweated four men at the air pumps, fast as the handles
   could go,
Forcing the air down that reached him, heated, and tainted,
   and slow—
Kanzo Makame the diver stayed seven minutes below;

Came up on deck like a dead man, paralysed body and
    brain;
Suffered, while blood was returning, infinite tortures of pain:
Sailed once again to the Darnleys—laughed and descended
    again!—

Scarce grew the shell in the shallows, rarely a patch could
    they touch;
Always the take was so little, always the labour so much;
Always they thought of the Islands held by the lumbering
    Dutch,

Islands where shell was in plenty lying in passage and bay,
Islands where divers could gather hundreds of shell in a
    day:
But the lumbering Dutch, with their gunboats, hunted the
    divers away.

Joe Nagasaki, the 'tender', finding the profits grow small,
Said, 'Let us go to the Islands, try for a number one haul!
If we get caught, go to prison—let them take lugger and all!'

Kanzo Makame, the diver—knowing full well what it
    meant—
Fatalist, gambler, and stoic, smiled a broad smile of content,
Flattened in mainsail and foresail, and off to the Islands they
    went.

Close to the headlands they drifted, picking up shell by the
    ton,
Piled up on deck were the oysters, opening wide in the sun,
When, from the lee of the headland, boomed the report of a
    gun.

Once that the diver was sighted, pearl shell and lugger must
    go.
Joe Nagasaki decided—quick was the word and the blow—
Cut both the pipe and the life line, leaving the diver below!

Kanzo Makame, the diver, failing to quite understand,
Pulled the 'haul up' on the life line, found it was slack in his
hand;
Then, like a little brown stoic, lay down and died on the
sand.

Joe Nagasaki, the 'tender', smiling a sanctified smile,
Headed her straight for the gunboat—throwing out shells all
the while—
Then went aboard and reported, 'No makee dive in three
mile!

'Dress no have got and no helmet—diver go shore on the
spree;
Plenty wind come and break rudder—lugger get blown out
to sea:
Take me to Japanee Consul, he help a poor Japanee!'

So the Dutch let him go, and they watched him, as off from
the Islands he ran,
Doubting him much, but what would you? You have to be
sure of your man
Ere you wake up that nest full of hornets—the little brown
men of Japan.

Down in the ooze and the coral, down where earth's
wonders are spread,
Helmeted, ghastly, and swollen, Kanzo Makame lies dead:
Joe Nagasaki, his 'tender', is owner and diver instead.

Wearer of pearls in your necklace, comfort yourself if you
can,
These are the risks of the pearling—these are the ways of
Japan,
'Plenty more Japanee diver, plenty more little brown man!'

The City of Dreadful Thirst

The stranger came from Narromine and made his little
    joke—
'They say we folks in Narromine are narrow-minded folk.
But all the smartest men down here are puzzled to define
A kind of new phenomenon that came to Narromine.

'Last summer up in Narromine 'twas gettin' rather warm—
Two hundred in the water bag, and lookin' like a storm—
We all were in the private bar, the coolest place in town,
When out across the stretch of plain a cloud came rollin' down,

'We don't respect the clouds up there, they fill us with disgust,
They mostly bring a Bogan shower—three raindrops and
    some dust;
But each man, simultaneous-like, to each man said, 'I think
That cloud suggests it's up to us to have another drink!'

'There's clouds of rain and clouds of dust—we'd heard of
    them before,
And sometimes in the daily press we read of "clouds of war":
But—if this ain't the Gospel truth I hope that I may burst—
That cloud that came to Narromine was just a cloud of thirst.

'It wasn't like a common cloud, 'twas more a sort of haze;
It settled down about the streets, and stopped for days and
    days,
And not a drop of dew could fall and not a sunbeam shine
To pierce that dismal sort of mist that hung on Narromine.

'Oh, Lord! we had a dreadful time beneath that cloud of thirst!
We all chucked-up our daily work and went upon the burst.
The very blacks about the town that used to cadge for grub,
They made an organised attack and tried to loot the pub.

'We couldn't leave the private bar no matter how we tried;
Shearers and squatters, union men and blacklegs side by side

Were drinkin' there and dursn't move, for each was sure, he
said,
Before he'd get a half a mile the thirst would strike him
dead!

'We drank until the drink gave out, we searched from room
to room,
And round the pub, like drunken ghosts, went howling
through the gloom.
The shearers found some kerosene and settled down again,
But all the squatter chaps and I, we staggered to the train.

'And, once outside the cloud of thirst, we felt as right as pie,
But while we stopped about the town we had to drink or die.
But now I hear it's safe enough, I'm going back to work
Because they say the cloud of thirst has shifted on to
Bourke.

'But when you see those clouds about—like this one over
here—
All white and frothy at the top, just like a pint of beer,
It's time to go and have a drink, for if that cloud should
burst
You'd find the drink would all be gone, for that's a cloud of
thirst!'

We stood the man from Narromine a pint of half-and-half;
He drank it off without a gasp in one tremendous quaff;
'I joined some friends last night,' he said, 'in what *they* called
a spree;
But after Narromine 'twas just a holiday to me.'

And now beyond the Western Range, where sunset skies are
red,
And clouds of dust, and clouds of thirst, go drifting
overhead,
The railway train is taking back, along the Western Line,
That narrow-minded person on his road to Narromine.

Hay and Hell and Booligal

'You come and see me, boys,' he said;
'You'll find a welcome and a bed
   And whisky any time you call;
Although our township hasn't got
The name of quite a lively spot—
   You see, I live in Booligal.

'And people have an awful down
Upon the district and the town—
   Which worse than hell itself they call;
In fact, the saying far and wide
Along the Riverina side
   Is "Hay and Hell and Booligal".

'No doubt it suits 'em very well
To say it's worse than Hay or Hell,
   But don't you heed their talk at all;
Of course, there's heat—no one denies—
And sand and dust and stacks of flies,
   And rabbits, too, at Booligal.

'But such a pleasant, quiet place,
You never see a stranger's face—
   They hardly ever care to call;
The drovers mostly pass it by;
They reckon that they'd rather die
   Than spend a night in Booligal.

'The big mosquitoes frighten some—
You'll lie awake to hear 'em hum—
   And snakes about the township crawl;
But shearers, when they get their cheque,
They never come along and wreck
   The blessed town of Booligal.

'But down in Hay the shearers come
And fill themselves with fighting rum,
    And chase blue devils up the wall,
And fight the snaggers every day,
Until there is the deuce to pay—
    There's none of that in Booligal.

'Of course, there isn't much to see—
The billiard table used to be
    The great attraction for us all,
Until some careless, drunken curs
Got sleeping on it in their spurs,
    And ruined it, in Booligal.

'Just now there is a howling drought
That pretty near has starved us out—
    It never seems to rain at all;
But, if there *should* come any rain,
You couldn't cross the black soil plain—
    You'd have to stop in Booligal.'

'*We'd have to stop*!' With bated breath
We prayed that both in life and death
    Our fate in other lines might fall:
'Oh, send us to our just reward
In Hay or Hell, but, gracious Lord,
    Deliver us from Booligal!'

A Walgett Episode

The sun strikes down with a blinding glare,
  The skies are blue and the plains are wide,
The saltbush plains that are burnt and bare
  By Walgett out on the Barwon side—
The Barwon River that wanders down
In a leisurely manner by Walgett Town.

There came a stranger—a 'cockatoo'—
  The word means farmer, as all men know
Who dwell in the land where the kangaroo
  Barks loud at dawn, and the white-eyed crow
Uplifts his song on the stockyard fence
As he watches the lambkins passing hence.

The sunburnt stranger was gaunt and brown,
  But it soon appeared that he meant to flout
The iron law of the country town,
  Which is—that the stranger has got to shout:
'If he will not shout we must take him down,'
Remarked the yokels of Walgett Town.

They baited a trap with a crafty bait,
  With a crafty bait, for they held discourse
Concerning a new chum who of late
  Had bought such a thoroughly lazy horse;
They would wager that no one could ride him down
The length of the city of Walgett Town.

The stranger was born on a horse's hide;
  So he took the wagers, and made them good
With his hard-earned cash—but his hopes they died,
  For the horse was a clothes-horse, made of wood!
'Twas a well-known horse that had taken down
Full many a stranger in Walgett Town.

The stranger smiled with a sickly smile—
    'Tis a sickly smile that the loser grins—
And he said he had travelled for quite a while
    In trying to sell some marsupial skins.
'And I thought that perhaps, as you've took me down,
You would buy them from me, in Walgett Town!'

He said that his home was at Wingadee,
    At Wingadee where he had for sale
Some fifty skins and would guarantee
    They were full-sized skins, with the ears and tail
Complete, and he sold them for money down
    To a venturesome buyer in Walgett Town.

Then he smiled a smile as he pouched the pelf,
    'I'm glad that I'm quit of them, win or lose:
You can fetch them in when it suits yourself,
    And you'll find the skins—on the kangaroos!'
Then he left—and the silence settled down
Like a tangible thing upon Walgett Town.

Father Riley's Horse

'Twas the horse thief, Andy Regan, that was hunted like a
    dog
  By the troopers of the upper Murray side,
They had searched in every gully—they had looked in every
    log,
  But never sight or track of him they spied,
Till the priest at Kiley's Crossing heard a knocking very late
  And a whisper 'Father Riley—come across!'
So his Rev'rence in pyjamas trotted softly to the gate
  And admitted Andy Regan—and a horse!

'Now, it's listen, Father Riley, to the words I've got to say,
  For it's close upon my death I am tonight.
With the troopers hard behind me I've been hiding all the
    day
  In the gullies keeping close and out of sight.
But they're watching all the ranges till there's not a bird
    could fly,
  And I'm fairly worn to pieces with the strife,
So I'm taking no more trouble, but I'm going home to die,
  'Tis the only way I see to save my life.

'Yes, I'm making home to mother's, and I'll die o' Tuesday
    next
  An' be buried on the Thursday—and, of course,
I'm prepared to meet my penance, but with one thing I'm
    perplexed
  And it's—Father, it's this jewel of a horse!
He was never bought nor paid for, and there's not a man
    can swear
  To his owner or his breeder, but I know,
That his sire was by Pedantic from the Old Pretender mare
  And his dam was close related to The Roe.

'And there's nothing in the district that can race him for a
    step,
  He could canter while they're going at their top:
He's the king of all the leppers that was ever seen to lep,
  A five-foot fence—he'd clear it in a hop!
So I'll leave him with you, Father, till the dead shall rise
    again,
  'Tis yourself that knows a good 'un; and, of course,
You can say he's got by Moonlight out of Paddy Murphy's
    plain
  If you're ever asked the breeding of the horse!

'But it's getting on to daylight and it's time to say goodbye,
  For the stars above the east are growing pale.
And I'm making home to mother—and it's hard for me to
    die!
  But it's harder still, is keeping out of gaol!
You can ride the old horse over to my grave across the dip
  Where the wattle bloom is waving overhead.
Sure he'll jump them fences easy—you must never raise the
    whip
  Or he'll rush 'em!—now, goodbye!' and he had fled!

So they buried Andy Regan, and they buried him to rights,
  In the graveyard at the back of Kiley's Hill;
There were five-and-twenty mourners who had five-and-
    twenty fights
  Till the very boldest fighters had their fill.
There were fifty horses racing from the graveyard to the
    pub,
  And their riders flogged each other all the while.
And the lashin's of the liquor! And the lavin's of the grub!
  Oh, poor Andy went to rest in proper style.

Then the races came to Kiley's—with a steeplechase and all,
  For the folk were mostly Irish round about,
And it takes an Irish rider to be fearless of a fall,
  They were training morning in and morning out.

But they never started training till the sun was on the
    course
  For a superstitious story kept 'em back,
That the ghost of Andy Regan on a slashing chestnut horse,
  Had been training by the starlight on the track.

And they read the nominations for the races with surprise
  And amusement at the Father's little joke,
For a novice had been entered for the steeplechasing prize,
  And they found that it was Father Riley's moke!
He was neat enough to gallop, he was strong enough to
    stay!
  But his owner's views of training were immense,
For the Reverend Father Riley used to ride him every day,
  And he never saw a hurdle nor a fence.

And the priest would join the laughter: 'Oh,' said he, 'I put
    him in,
  For there's five-and-twenty sovereigns to be won.
And the poor would find it useful, if the chestnut chanced
    to win,
  And he'll maybe win when all is said and done!'
He had called him Faugh-a-ballagh, which is French for
    'clear the course',
  And his colours were a vivid shade of green:
All the Dooleys and O'Donnells were on Father Riley's
    horse,
  While the Orangemen were backing Mandarin!

It was Hogan, the dog poisoner—aged man and very wise,
  Who was camping in the racecourse with his swag,
And who ventured the opinion, to the township's great
    surprise,
  That the race would go to Father Riley's nag.
'You can talk about your riders—and the horse has not been
    schooled,
  And the fences is terrific, and the rest!

When the field is fairly going, then ye'll see ye've all been
  fooled,
  And the chestnut horse will battle with the best.

'For there's some has got condition, and they think the race
  is sure,
  And the chestnut horse will fall beneath the weight,
But the hopes of all the helpless, and the prayers of all the
  poor,
  Will be running by his side to keep him straight.
And it's what's the need of schoolin' or of workin' on the
  track,
  Whin the saints are there to guide him round the course!
I've prayed him over every fence—I've prayed him out and
  back!
  And I'll bet my cash on Father Riley's horse!'

Oh, the steeple was a caution! They went tearin' round and
  round,
  And the fences rang and rattled where they struck.
There was some that cleared the water—there was more fell
  in and drowned,
  Some blamed the men and others blamed the luck!
But the whips were flying freely when the field came into
  view,
  For the finish down the long green stretch of course,
And in front of all the flyers—jumpin' like a kangaroo,
  Came the rank outsider—Father Riley's horse!

Oh, the shouting and the cheering as he rattled past the
  post!
  For he left the others standing, in the straight;
And the rider—well they reckoned it was Andy Regan's
  ghost,
  And it beat 'em how a ghost would draw the weight!
But he weighed in, nine stone seven, then he laughed and
  disappeared,
  Like a banshee (which is Spanish for an elf),

80

And old Hogan muttered sagely, 'If it wasn't for the beard
   They'd be thinking it was Andy Regan's self!'

And the poor of Kiley's Crossing drank the health at
      Christmastide
   Of the chestnut and his rider dressed in green.
There was never such a rider, not since Andy Regan died,
   And they wondered who on earth he could have been.
But they settled it among 'em, for the story got about,
   'Mongst the bushmen and the people on the course,
That the Devil had been ordered to let Andy Regan out
   For the steeplechase on Father Riley's horse!

Song of the Artesian Water

Now the stock have started dying, for the Lord has sent a
    drought;
But we're sick of prayers and Providence—we're going to do
    without;
With the derricks up above us and the solid earth below,
We are waiting at the lever for the word to let her go.
    Sinking down, deeper down,
    Oh, we'll sink it deeper down:
As the drill is plugging downward at a thousand feet of
    level,
If the Lord won't send us water, oh, we'll get it from the
    devil;
    Yes, we'll get it from the devil deeper down.

Now, our engine's built in Glasgow by a very canny Scot,
And he marked it twenty horsepower, but he don't know
    what is what:
When Canadian Bill is firing with the sun-dried gidgee logs,
She can equal thirty horses and a score or so of dogs.
    Sinking down, deeper down,
    Oh, we're going deeper down:
If we fail to get the water then it's ruin to the squatter,
For the drought is on the station and the weather's growing
    hotter,
    But we're bound to get the water deeper down.

But the shaft has started caving and the sinking's very slow,
And the yellow rods are bending in the water down below,
And the tubes are always jamming and they can't be made
    to shift
Till we nearly burst the engine with a forty horsepower lift.
    Sinking down, deeper down
    Oh, we going deeper down:
Though the shaft is always caving, and the tubes are always
    jamming,

Yet we'll fight our way to water while the stubborn drill is
     ramming—
  While the stubborn drill is ramming deeper down.

But there's no artesian water, though we've passed three
     thousand feet,
And the contract price is growing and the boss is nearly
     beat.
But it must be down beneath us, and it's down we've got to
     go,
Though she's bumping on the solid rock four thousand feet
     below.
  Sinking down, deeper down,
  Oh, we're going deeper down:
And it's time they heard us knocking on the roof of Satan's
     dwellin';
But we'll get artesian water if we cave the roof of Hell in—
  Oh! we'll get artesian water deeper down.

But it's hark! the whistle's blowing with a wild, exultant
     blast,
And the boys are madly cheering, for they've struck the
     flow at last,
And it's rushing up the tubing from four thousand feet
     below
Till it spouts above the casing in a million-gallon flow.
  And it's down, deeper down,
  Oh, it comes from deeper down;
It is flowing, ever flowing, in a free, unstinted measure
From the silent hidden places where the old earth hides her
     treasure—
  Where the old earth hides her treasure deeper down.

And it's clear away the timber, and it's let the water run:
How it glimmers in the shadow, how it flashes in the sun!
By the silent belts of timber, by the miles of blazing plain
It is bringing hope and comfort to the thirsty land again.
  Flowing down, further down;
  It is flowing further down

To the tortured thirsty cattle, bringing gladness in its going;
Through the droughty days of summer it is flowing, ever
    flowing—
  It is flowing, ever flowing, further down.

The Road to Gundagai

The mountain road goes up and down,
From Gundagai to Tumut town.

And branching off there runs a track,
Across the foothills grim and black,

Across the plains and ranges grey
To Sydney city far away.

It came by chance one day that I
From Tumut rode to Gundagai.

And reached about the evening tide
The crossing where the roads divide;

And, waiting at the crossing place,
I saw a maiden fair of face,

With eyes of deepest violet blue,
And cheeks to match the rose in hue—

The fairest maids Australia knows
Are bred among the mountain snows.

Then, fearing I might go astray,
I asked if she could show the way.

Her voice might well a man bewitch—
Its tones so supple, deep, and rich.

'The tracks are clear,' she made reply,
'And this goes down to Sydney town,
And that one goes to Gundagai.'

Then slowly, looking coyly back,
She went along the Sydney track.

And I for one was well content
To go the road the lady went;

But round the turn a swain she met—
The kiss she gave him haunts me yet!

I turned and travelled with a sigh
The lonely road to Gundagai.

The Old Australian Ways

The London lights are far abeam
    Behind a bank of cloud,
Along the shore the gas lights gleam,
    The gale is piping loud;
And down the Channel, groping blind,
    We drive her through the haze
Towards the land we left behind—
The good old land of 'never mind',
    And old Australian ways.

The narrow ways of English folk
    Are not for such as we;
They bear the long-accustomed yoke
    Of staid conservancy:
But all our roads are new and strange
    And through our blood there runs
The vagabonding love of change
That drove us westward of the range
    And westward of the suns.

The city folk go to and fro
    Behind a prison's bars,
They never feel the breezes blow
    And never see the stars;
They never hear in blossomed trees
    The music low and sweet
Of wild birds making melodies
Nor catch the little laughing breeze
    That whispers in the wheat.

Our fathers came of roving stock
    That could not fixed abide:
And we have followed field and flock
    Since e'er we learnt to ride;
By miner's camp and shearing shed,
    In land of heat and drought,

We followed where our fortunes led,
With fortune always on ahead
   And always further out.

The wind is in the barley grass,
   The wattles are in bloom;
The breezes greet us as they pass
   With honey-sweet perfume;
The parakeets go screaming by
   With flash of golden wing,
And from the swamp the wild ducks cry
Their long-drawn note of revelry,
   Rejoicing at the spring.

So throw the weary pen aside
   And let the papers rest,
For we must saddle up and ride
   Towards the blue hill's breast;
And we must travel far and fast
   Across their rugged maze,
To find the Spring of Youth at last,
And call back from the buried past
   The old Australian ways.

When Clancy took the drover's track
   In years of long ago,
He drifted to the outer back
   Beyond the Overflow;
By rolling plain and rocky shelf,
   With stockwhip in his hand,
He reached at last, oh lucky elf,
The Town of Come-and-Help-Yourself
   In Rough-and-Ready Land.

And if it be that you would know
   The tracks he used to ride,
Then you must saddle up and go
   Beyond the Queensland side—

Beyond the reach of rule or law,
    To ride the long day through,
In Nature's homestead—filled with awe:
You then might see what Clancy saw
    And know what Clancy knew.

It's Grand

It's grand to be a squatter
   And sit upon a post,
And watch your little ewes and lambs
   A-giving up the ghost.

It's grand to be a 'cockie'
   With wife and kids to keep,
And find an all-wise Providence
   Has mustered all your sheep.

It's grand to be a western man,
   With shovel in your hand,
To dig your little homestead out
   From underneath the sand.

It's grand to be a shearer,
   Along the Darling side,
And pluck the wool from stinking sheep
   That some days since have died.

It's grand to be a rabbit
   And breed till all is blue,
And then to die in heaps because
   There's nothing left to chew.

It's grand to be a Minister
   And travel like a swell,
And tell the central district folk
   To go to—Inverell.

It's grand to be a Socialist
   And lead the bold array
That marches to prosperity
   At seven bob a day.

It's grand to be an unemployed
    And lie in the Domain,
And wake up every second day
    And go to sleep again.

It's grand to borrow English tin
    To pay for wharves and Rocks,
And then to find it isn't in
    The little money-box.

It's grand to be a democrat
    And toady to the mob,
For fear that if you told the truth
    They'd hunt you from your job.

It's grand to be a lot of things
    In this fair southern land,
But if the Lord would send us rain,
    That would, indeed, be grand!

The Road to Old Man's Town

The fields of youth are filled with flowers,
   The wine of youth is strong:
What need have we to count the hours?
   The summer days are long.

But soon we find to our dismay
   That we are drifting down
The barren slopes that fall away
Towards the foothills grim and grey
   That lead to Old Man's Town.

And marching with us on the track
   Full many friends we find:
We see them looking sadly back
   For those that dropped behind.

But God forbid a fate so dread—
   Alone to travel down
The dreary road we all must tread,
With faltering steps and whitening head,
   The road to Old Man's Town!

Driver Smith

'Twas Driver Smith of Battery A was anxious to see a fight;
He thought of the Transvaal all the day, he thought of it all
    the night—
'Well, if the battery's left behind, I'll go to the war,' says he,
'I'll go a-driving an ambulance in the ranks of the A.M.C.

'I'm fairly sick of these here parades, it's want of a change
    that kills
A-charging the Randwick Rifle Range and aiming at Surry
    Hills.
And I think if I go with the ambulance I'm certain to find a
    show,
For they have to send the medical men wherever the troops
    can go.

'Wherever the rifle bullets flash and the Maxims raise a din,
It's there you'll find the medical men a-raking the wounded
    in—
A-raking 'em in like human flies—and a driver smart like me
Will find some scope for his extra skill in the ranks of the
    A.M.C.'

So Driver Smith he went to the war a-cracking his driver's
    whip,
From ambulance to collecting base they showed him his
    regular trip.
And he said to the boys that were marching past, as he gave
    his whip a crack,
'You'll walk yourselves to the fight,' says he—'Lord spare
    me, I'll drive you back.'

Now, the fight went on in the Transvaal hills for the half of a
    day or more,
And Driver Smith he worked his trip—all aboard for the seat
    of war!

He took his load from the stretcher men and hurried 'em
    homeward fast
Till he heard a sound that he knew full well—a battery
    rolling past.

He heard the clink of the leading chains and the roll of the
    guns behind—
He heard the crack of the drivers' whips, and he says to 'em,
    'Strike me blind,
I'll miss me trip with this ambulance, although I don't care
    to shirk,
But I'll take the car off the line to-day and follow the guns at
    work.'

Then up the Battery Colonel came a-cursing 'em black in the
    face.
'Sit down and shift 'em, you drivers there, and gallop 'em
    into place.'
So off the Battery rolled and swung, a-going a merry dance,
And holding his own with the leading gun goes Smith with
    his ambulance.

They opened fire on the mountainside, a-peppering by and
    large,
When over the hill above their flank the Boers came down
    at the charge;
They rushed the guns with a daring rush, a-volleying left
    and right,
And Driver Smith with his ambulance moved up to the
    edge of the fight.

The gunners stuck to their guns like men, and fought like
    the wild cats fight,
For a Battery man don't leave his gun with ever a hope in
    sight;
But the bullets sang and the Mausers cracked and the
    Battery men gave way,
Till Driver Smith with his ambulance drove into the thick of
    the fray.

He saw the head of the Transvaal troop a-thundering to and
    fro,
A hard old face with a monkey beard—a face that he
    seemed to know;
'Now, who's that leader,' said Driver Smith, 'I've seen him
    before to-day.
Why, bless my heart, but it's Kruger's self,' and he jumped
    for him straight away.

He collared old Kruger round the waist and hustled him
    into the van.
It wasn't according to stretcher drill for raising a wounded
    man;
But he forced him in and said: 'All aboard, we're off for a
    little ride,
And you'll have the car to yourself,' says he, 'I reckon we're
    full inside.'

He wheeled his team on the mountainside and set 'em a
    merry pace,
A-galloping over the rocks and stones, and a lot of the Boers
    gave chase;
But Driver Smith had a fairish start, and he said to the
    Boers, 'Good-day,
You have Buckley's chance for to catch a man that was
    trained in Battery A.'

He drove his team to the hospital and said to the P.M.O.,
'Beg pardon, sir, but I missed a trip, mistaking the way to
    go;
And Kruger came to the ambulance and asked could we
    spare a bed,
So I fetched him here, and we'll take him home to show for a
    bob a head.'

So the word went round to the English troops to say they
    need fight no more,
For Driver Smith with his ambulance had ended the
    blooming war:

And in London now at the music halls he's starring it every
   night,
And drawing a hundred pounds a week to tell how he won
   the fight.

On the Trek

Oh, the weary, weary journey on the trek, day after day,
  With sun above and silent veldt below;
And our hearts keep turning homeward to the youngsters
    far away,
  And the homestead where the climbing roses grow.
Shall we see the flats grow golden with the ripening of the
    grain?
  Shall we hear the parrots calling on the bough?
Ah! the weary months of marching ere we hear them call
    again,
  For we're going on a long job now.

In the drowsy days on escort, riding slowly half asleep,
  With the endless line of waggons stretching back,
While the khaki soldiers travel like a mob of travelling
    sheep,
  Plodding silent on the never-ending track,
While the constant snap and sniping of the foe you never
    see
  Makes you wonder will your turn come—when and how?
As the Mauser ball hums past you like a vicious kind of
    bee—
  Oh! we're going on a long job now.

When the dash and the excitement and the novelty are
    dead,
  And you've seen a load of wounded once or twice,
Or you've watched your old mate dying—with the vultures
    overhead,
  Well, you wonder if the war is worth the price.
And down along Monaro now they're starting out to shear,
  I can picture the excitement and the row;
But they'll miss me on the Lachlan when they call the roll
    this year,
  For we're going on a long job now.

Johnny Boer

Men fight all shapes and sizes as the racing horses run,
And no man knows his courage till he stands before a gun.
At mixed-up fighting, hand to hand, and clawing men about
They reckon Fuzzy-wuzzy is the hottest fighter out.
But Fuzzy gives himself away—his style is out of date,
He charges like a driven grouse that rushes on its fate;
You've nothing in the world to do but pump him full of
    lead:
But when you're fighting Johnny Boer you have to use your
    head;
He don't believe in front attacks or charging at the run,
He fights you from a kopje with his little Maxim gun.

For when the Lord He made the earth, it seems uncommon
    clear,
He gave the job of Africa to some good engineer,
Who started building fortresses on fashions of his own—
Lunettes, redoubts, and counterscarps all made of rock and
    stone.
The Boer needs only bring a gun, for ready to his hand
He finds these heaven-built fortresses all scattered through
    the land;
And there he sits and winks his eye and wheels his gun
    about,
And we must charge across the plain to hunt the beggar
    out.
It ain't a game that grows on us, there's lots of better fun
Than charging at old Johnny with his little Maxim gun.

On rocks a goat could scarcely climb, steep as the walls of
    Troy,
He wheels a four-point-seven about as easy as a toy;
With bullocks yoked and drag ropes manned, he lifts her up
    the rocks
And shifts her every now and then, as cunning as a fox.

At night you mark her right ahead, you see her clean and
   clear,
Next day at dawn—'What, ho! she bumps'—from
   somewhere in the rear.
Or else the keenest-eyed patrol will miss him with the glass—
He's lying hidden in the rocks to let the leaders pass;
But when the main guard comes along he opens up the fun,
There's lots of ammunition for the little Maxim gun.

But after all the job is sure, although the job is slow,
We have to see the business through, the Boer has got to go.
With Nordenfeldt and lyddite shell it's certain, soon or late,
We'll hunt him from his kopjes and across the Orange State;
And then across those open flats you'll see the beggar run,
And we'll be running after with *our* little Maxim gun.

Right in Front of the Army

'Where 'ave you been this week or more,
'Aven't seen you about the war?
Thought perhaps you was at the rear
Guarding the waggons.' 'What, us? No fear!
Where have we been? Why, bless my heart,
Where have we been since the bloomin' start?
    Right in the front of the army,
      Battling day and night!
    Right in the front of the army,
      Teaching 'em how to fight!'
    Every separate man you see,
    Sapper, gunner, and C.I.V.,
    Every one of 'em seems to be
    Right in the front of the army!

Most of the troops to the camp had gone,
When we met with a cow gun toiling on;
And we said to the boys, as they walked her past,
'Well, thank goodness, you're here at last!'
'Here at last! Why, what d'yer mean?
Ain't we just where we've always been?
    Right in the front of the army,
      Battling day and night!
    Right in the front of the army,
      Teaching 'em how to fight!'
    Correspondents and vets in force,
    Mounted foot and dismounted horse,
    All of them were, as a matter of course,
    Right in the front of the army.

Old Lord Roberts will have to mind
If ever the enemy get behind;
For they'll smash him up with a rear attack,
Because his army has got no back!
Think of the horrors that might befall
An army without any rear at all!

Right in the front of the army,
    Battling day and night!
Right in the front of the army,
    Teaching 'em how to fight!
Swede attachés and German counts,
Yeomen (known as De Wet's remounts),
All of them were by their own accounts
Right in the front of the army!

Song of the Wheat

We have sung the song of the droving days,
    Of the march of the travelling sheep;
By silent stages and lonely ways
    Thin, white battalions creep.
But the man who now by the land would thrive
    Must his spurs to a ploughshare beat.
Is there ever a man in the world alive
    To sing the song of the Wheat!

It's west by south of the Great Divide
    The grim grey plains run out,
Where the old flock masters lived and died
    In a ceaseless fight with drought.
Weary with waiting and hope deferred
    They were ready to own defeat,
Till at last they heard the master-word
    And the master-word was Wheat.

Yarran and Myall and Box and Pine—
    'Twas axe and fire for all;
They scarce could tarry to blaze the line
    Or wait for the trees to fall,
Ere the team was yoked and the gates flung wide,
    And the dust of the horses' feet
Rose up like a pillar of smoke to guide
    The wonderful march of Wheat.

Furrow by furrow, and fold by fold,
    The soil is turned on the plain;
Better than silver and better than gold
    Is the surface-mine of the grain.
Better than cattle and better than sheep
    In the fight with the drought and heat.
For a streak of stubbornness wide and deep
    Lies hid in a grain of Wheat.

When the stock is swept by the hand of fate,
    Deep down in his bed of clay
The brave brown Wheat will lie and wait
    For the resurrection day:
Lie hid while the whole world thinks him dead;
    But the spring rain, soft and sweet,
Will over the steaming paddocks spread
    The first green flush of the Wheat.

Green and amber and gold it grows
    When the sun sinks late in the West
And the breeze sweeps over the rippling rows
    Where the quail and the skylark nest.
Mountain or river or shining star,
    There's never a sight can beat—
Away to the skyline stretching far—
    A sea of the ripening Wheat.

When the burning harvest sun sinks low,
    And the shadows stretch on the plain,
The roaring strippers come and go
    Like ships on a sea of grain;
Till the lurching, groaning waggons bear
    Their tale of the load complete.
Of the world's great work he has done his share
    Who has gathered a crop of wheat.

Princes and Potentates and Czars,
    They travel in regal state,
But old King Wheat has a thousand cars
    For his trip to the water-gate;
And his thousand steamships breast the tide
    And plough thro' the wind and sleet
To the lands where the teeming millions bide
    That say, 'Thank God for Wheat!'

Brumby's Run

The Aboriginal term for a wild horse is 'brumby'. At a recent trial in Sydney a Supreme Court Judge, hearing of 'brumby horses', asked 'Who is Brumby, and where is his run?'

It lies beyond the western pines
   Towards the sinking sun,
And not a survey mark defines
   The bounds of 'Brumby's run'.

On odds and ends of mountain land
   On tracks of range and rock,
Where no one else can make a stand,
   Old Brumby rears his stock—

A wild, unhandled lot they are
   Of every shape and breed,
They venture out 'neath moon and star
   Along the flats to feed.

But when the dawn makes pink the sky
   And steals along the plain,
The Brumby horses turn and fly
   Towards the hills again.

The traveller by the mountain track
   May hear their hoofbeats pass,
And catch a glimpse of brown and black,
   Dim shadows on the grass.

The eager stock horse pricks his ears
   And lifts his head on high
In wild excitement when he hears
   The Brumby mob go by.

Old Brumby asks no price or fee
  O'er all his wide domains:
The man who yards his stock is free
  To keep them for his pains.

So, off to scour the mountainside
  With eager eyes aglow,
To strongholds where the wild mobs hide
  The gully-rakers go.

Saltbush Bill, J.P.

Beyond the land where Leichhardt went,
  Beyond Sturt's western track,
The rolling tide of change has sent
  Some strange J.P.s out back.

And Saltbush Bill, grown old and grey,
  And worn with want of sleep,
Received the news in camp one day
  Behind the travelling sheep,

That Edward Rex, confiding in
  His known integrity,
By hand and seal on parchment skin
  Had made him a J.P.

He read the news with eager face
  But found no word of pay.
'I'd like to see my sister's place
  And kids on Christmas Day.

'I'd like to see green grass again,
  And watch clear water run,
Away from this unholy plain,
  And flies, and dust, and sun.'

At last one little clause he found
  That might some hope inspire,
'A magistrate may charge a pound
  For inquest on a fire.'

A big blacks' camp was built close by
  And Saltbush Bill, says he,
'I think that camp might well supply
  A job for a J.P.'

That night, by strange coincidence,
    A most disastrous fire
Destroyed the country residence
    Of Jacky Jack, Esquire.

'Twas mostly leaves, and bark, and dirt;
    The party most concerned
Appeared to think it wouldn't hurt
    If forty such were burned.

Quite otherwise thought Saltbush Bill,
    Who watched the leaping flame.
'The home is small,' said he, 'but still
    The principle's the same.

''Midst palaces though you should roam,
    Or follow pleasure's tracks,
You'll find,' he said, 'no place like home,
    At least like Jacky Jack's.

'Tell every man in camp "Come quick",
    Tell every black Maria,
I give tobacco half a stick—
    Hold inquest long-a fire.'

Each juryman received a name
    Well suited to a Court.
'Long Jack' and 'Stumpy Bill' became
    'John Long' and 'William Short'.

While such as 'Tarpot', 'Bullock Dray',
    And 'Tommy Wait-a-While',
Became, for ever and a day,
    'Scott', 'Dickens', and 'Carlyle'.

And twelve good sable men and true
    Were soon engaged upon
The conflagration that o'erthrew
    The home of John A. John.

Their verdict, 'Burnt by act of fate',
   They scarcely had returned
When, just behind the magistrate,
   Another humpy burned!

The jury sat again and drew
   Another stick of plug.
Said Saltbush Bill, 'It's up to you
   Put some one long-a jug.'

'I'll camp the sheep,' he said, 'and shift
   The evidence about.'
For quite a week he couldn't shift,
   The way the fires broke out.

The jury thought the whole concern
   As good as any play.
They used to 'take him oath' and earn
   Three sticks of plug a day.

At last the tribe lay down to sleep
   Homeless, beneath a tree;
And onward with his travelling sheep
   Went Saltbush Bill, J.P.

The sheep delivered, safe and sound,
   His horse to town he turned,
And drew some five-and-twenty pound
   For fees that he had earned.

And where Monaro's ranges hide
   Their little farms away,
His sister's children by his side,
   He spent his Christmas Day.

The next J.P. that went outback
   Was shocked, or pained, or both
At hearing every pagan black
   Repeat the juror's oath.

No matter though he turned and fled
    They followed faster still,
'You make it inkwich, boss,' they said
    'All same like Saltbush Bill.'

They even said they'd let him see
    The fires originate.
When he refused they said that he
    Was 'No good magistrate'.

And out beyond Sturt's Western track,
    And Leichhardt's furthest tree,
They wait till fate shall send them back
    Their Saltbush Bill, J.P.

Waltzing Matilda

Carrying a Swag

Oh there once was a swagman camped in the billabongs,
    Under the shade of a Coolibah tree;
And he sang as he looked at the old billy boiling,
    'Who'll come a-waltzing Matilda with me.'

    Who'll come a-waltzing Matilda, my darling,
        Who'll come a-waltzing Matilda with me.
    Waltzing Matilda and leading a water-bag,
        Who'll come a-waltzing Matilda with me.

Up came the jumbuck to drink at the waterhole,
    Up jumped the swagman and grabbed him in glee;
And he sang as he put him away in his tucker-bag,
    'You'll come a-waltzing Matilda with me.'

    Who'll come a-waltzing Matilda, my darling,
        Who'll come a-waltzing Matilda with me.
    Waltzing Matilda and leading a water-bag,
        Who'll come a-waltzing Matilda with me.

Up came the squatter a-riding his thoroughbred;
    Up came policemen—one, two, and three.
'Whose is the jumbuck you've got in the tucker-bag?
    You'll come a-waltzing Matilda with we.'

    Who'll come a-waltzing Matilda, my darling,
        Who'll come a-waltzing Matilda with me.
    Waltzing Matilda and leading a water-bag,
        Who'll come a-waltzing Matilda with me.

Up sprang the swagman and jumped in the waterhole,
    Drowning himself by the Coolibah tree;
And his voice can be heard as it sings in the billabongs,
    'Who'll come a-waltzing Matilda with me?'

Who'll come a-waltzing Matilda, my darling,
  Who'll come a-waltzing Matilda with me.
Waltzing Matilda and leading a water-bag,
  Who'll come a-waltzing Matilda with me.

An Answer to Various Bards

Well, I've waited mighty patient while they all come rolling
  in,
Mister Lawson, Mister Dyson, and the others of their kin,
With their dreadful, dismal stories of the overlander's camp,
How his fire is always smoky, and his boots are always
  damp;
And they paint it so terrific it would fill one's soul with
  gloom,
But you know they're fond of writing about 'corpses' and
  'the tomb'
So, before they curse the bushland they should let their
  fancy range,
And take something for their livers, and be cheerful for a
  change.

Now, for instance, Mister Lawson—well, of course, we
  almost cried
At the sorrowful description how his 'little 'Arvie' died.
And we wept in silent sorrow when 'His Father's Mate' was
  slain;
Then he went and killed the father, and we had to weep
  again.
Ben Duggan and Jack Denver, too, he caused them to expire,
And he went and cooked the gander of Jack Dunn, of
  Nevertire;
And he spoke in terms prophetic of a revolution's beat,
When the world should hear the clamour of those people in
  the street;
But the shearer chaps who start it—why, he rounds on
  them in blame,
And he calls 'em 'agitators' who are living on the game.
So, no doubt, the bush is wretched if you judge it by the
  groan
Of the sad and soulful poet with a graveyard of his own.

But I 'over-write' the bushmen! Well, I own without a doubt
That I always see a hero in the 'man from furthest out'.
I could never contemplate him through an atmosphere of
    gloom,
And the bushman never struck me as a subject for 'the
    tomb'.
If it ain't all 'golden sunshine' where the 'wattle branches
    wave',
Well, it ain't all damp and dismal, and it ain't all 'lonely
    grave'.
And, of course, there's no denying that the bushman's life is
    rough,
But a man can easy stand it if he's built of sterling stuff;
Tho' it's seldom that the drover gets a bed of eiderdown,
Yet the man who's born a bushman, he gets mighty sick of
    town,
For he's jotting down the figures, and he's adding up the
    bills
While his heart is simply aching for a sight of southern hills.
Then he hears a wool team passing with a rumble and a
    lurch,
And although the work is pressing yet it brings him off his
    perch.
For it stirs him like a message from his station friends afar
And he seems to sniff the ranges in the scent of wool and
    tar;
And it takes him back in fancy, half in laughter, half in tears,
To a sound of other voices and a thought of other years,
When the woolshed rang with bustle from the dawning of
    the day,
And the shear blades were a-clicking to the cry of 'wool
    away!'
When his face was somewhat browner and his frame was
    firmer set,
And he feels his flabby muscles with a feeling of regret.
Then the wool team slowly passes and his eyes go sadly
    back
To the dusty little table and the papers in the rack,

And his thoughts go to the terrace where his sickly children
  squall,
And he thinks there's something healthy in the bush life
  after all.

But we'll go no more a-droving in the wind or in the sun,
For our fathers' hearts have failed us and the droving days
  are done.
There's a nasty dash of danger where the long-horned
  bullock wheels,
And we like to live in comfort and get our reg'lar meals.
And to hang about the townships suits us better, you'll agree,
For a job at washing bottles is the job for such as we.
Let us herd into the cities, let us crush and crowd and push
Till we lose the love of roving and we learn to hate the bush;
And we'll turn our aspirations to a city life and beer,
And we'll sneak across to England—it's a nicer place than
  here;
For there's not much risk of hardship where all comforts are
  in store,
And the theatres are plenty and the pubs are more and
  more.

But that ends it, Mister Lawson, and it's time to say
  good-bye,
We must agree to differ in all friendship, you and I;
And our personal opinions—well, they're scarcely worth a
  rush,
For there's some that like the city and there's some that like
  the bush;
And there's no one quite contented, as I've always heard it
  said,
Except one favoured person, and *he* turned out to be dead.
So we'll work our own salvation with the stoutest hearts we
  may,
And if fortune only favours we will take the road some day,
And go droving down the river 'neath the sunshine and the
  stars,
And then we'll come to Sydney and vermilionise the bars.

114

The Road to Hogan's Gap

Now look, y' see, it's this way like,
  Y' cross the broken bridge
And run the crick down till y' strike
  The second right-hand ridge.

The track is hard to see in parts,
  But still it's pretty clear;
There's been two Injin hawkers' carts
  Along that road this year.

Well, run that right-hand ridge along,
  It ain't, to say, too steep.
There's two fresh tracks might put y' wrong
  Where blokes went out with sheep.

But keep the crick upon your right,
  And follow pretty straight
Along the spur, until y' sight
  A wire and sapling gate.

Well, that's where Hogan's old grey mare
  Fell off and broke her back;
You'll see her carcase layin' there,
  Jist down below the track.

And then you drop two mile, or three,
  It's pretty steep and blind;
You want to go and fall a tree
  And tie it on behind.

And then you'll pass a broken cart
  Below a granite bluff;
And that is where you strike the part
  They reckon pretty rough.

But by the time you've got that far
    It's either cure or kill,
So turn your horses round the spur
    And face 'em up the hill.

For, look, if you should miss the slope
    And get below the track,
You haven't got the whitest hope
    Of ever gettin' back.

An' halfway up you'll see the hide
    Of Hogan's brindled bull;
Well, mind and keep the right-hand side,
    The left's too steep a pull.

And both the banks is full of cracks;
    An' just about at dark
You'll see the last year's bullock tracks
    Where Hogan drew the bark.

The marks is old and pretty faint
    And grown with scrub and such;
Of course the track to Hogan's ain't
    A road that's travelled much.

But turn and run the tracks along
    For half a mile or more,
And then, of course, you can't go wrong—
    You're right at Hogan's door.

When first you come to Hogan's gate
    He mightn't show, perhaps;
He's pretty sure to plant and wait
    To see it ain't the traps.

I wouldn't call it good enough
    To let your horses out;

There's some that's pretty extra rough
    Is livin' round about.

It's likely if your horses did
    Get feedin' near the track,
It's goin' to cost at least a quid
    Or more to get them back.

So, if you find they're off the place,
    It's up to you to go
And flash a quid in Hogan's face—
    He'll know the blokes that know.

But, listen, if you're feelin' dry,
    Just see there's no one near,
And go and wink the other eye
    And ask for ginger beer.

The blokes come in from near and far
    To sample Hogan's pop;
They reckon once they breast the bar
    They stay there till they drop.

On Sundays you can see them spread
    Like flies around the tap.
It's like that song 'The Livin' Dead'
    Up there at Hogan's Gap.

They like to make it pretty strong
    Whenever there's a charnce;
So when a stranger comes along
    They always holds a darnce.

There's recitations, songs, and fights,
    They do the thing a treat.
There's one long bloke up there recites
    As well as e'er you'd meet.

They're lively blokes all right up there,
    It's never dull a day.
I'd go meself if I could spare
    The time to get away.

The stranger turned his horses, quick,
    He didn't cross the bridge.
He didn't go along the crick
    To strike the second ridge.

He didn't make the trip, because
    He wasn't feeling fit.
His business up at Hogan's was
    To serve him with a writ.

He reckoned if he faced the pull
    And climbed the rocky stair,
The next to come might find his hide
A landmark on the mountain side,
Along with Hogan's brindled bull
    And Hogan's old grey mare!

Pioneers

They came of bold and roving stock that would not fixed
abide;
They were the sons of field and flock since e'er they learned
to ride;
We may not hope to see such men in these degenerate years
As those explorers of the bush—the brave old pioneers.

'Twas they who rode the trackless bush in heat and storm
and drought;
'Twas they that heard the master-word that called them
further out;
'Twas they that followed up the trail the mountain cattle
made
And pressed across the mighty range where now their
bones are laid.

But now the times are dull and slow, the brave old days are
dead
When hardy bushmen started out, and forced their way
ahead
By tangled scrub and forests grim towards the unknown
west,
And spied the far-off promised land from off the ranges'
crest.

Oh! ye, that sleep in lonely graves by far-off ridge and plain,
We drink to you in silence now as Christmas comes again,
The men who fought the wilderness through rough,
unsettled years—
The founders of our nation's life, the brave old pioneers.

Santa Claus in the Bush

It chanced out back at the Christmas time,
　　When the wheat was ripe and tall,
A stranger rode to the farmer's gate,
　　A sturdy man, and a small.

'Run down, run down, my little son Jack,
　　And bid the stranger stay;
And we'll hae a crack for the "Auld Lang Syne",
　　For tomorrow is Christmas Day.'

'Nay now, nay now,' said the dour gude wife,
　　'But ye should let him be;
He's maybe only a drover chap
　　From the land o' the Darling Pea.

'Wi' a drover's tales, and a drover's thirst
　　To swiggle the whole night through;
Or he's maybe a life assurance carle,
　　To talk ye black and blue.'

'Gude wife, he's never a drover chap,
　　For their swags are neat and thin;
And he's never a life assurance carle,
　　Wi' the brick dust burnt in his skin.

'Gude wife, gude wife, be not so dour,
　　For the wheat stands ripe and tall,
And we shore wi' a seven-pound fleece this year,
　　Ewes and weaners and all.

'There is grass to spare, and the stock are fat,
　　When they whiles are gaunt and thin,
And we owe a tithe to the travelling poor,
　　So we must ask him in.

'You can set him a chair to the table side,
    And give him a bite to eat;
An omelette made of a new-laid egg,
    Or a tasty piece of meat.'

'But the native cats have taken the fowls,
    They have na' left a leg;
And he'll get no omelette here at all
    Till the emu lays an egg!'

'Run down, run down, my little son Jack,
    To where the emus bide,
Ye shall find the old hen on the nest,
    While the old cock sits beside.

'But speak them fair, and speak them soft,
    Lest they kick ye a fearsome jolt,
Ye can give them a feed of thae half-inch nails,
    Or a rusty carriage bolt.'

So little son Jack ran blithely down,
    With the rusty nails in hand,
Till he came where the emus fluffed and scratched,
    By their nest in the open sand.

And there he has gathered the new-laid egg,
    Would feed three men or four,
And the emus came for the half-inch nails,
    Right up to the settler's door.

'A waste of food,' said the dour gude wife,
    As she took the egg, wi' a frown.
'But he gets no meat, unless ye run
    A paddymelon down.'

'Gae oot, gae oot, my little son Jack,
    Wi your twa-three doggies small;
Gin ye come not back wi' a paddymelon,
    Then come not back at all.'

So little son Jack he raced and he ran,
    And he was bare o' the feet,
And soon he captured the paddymelon,
    Was gorged wi' the stolen wheat.

'Sit down, sit down, my bonny wee man,
    To the best that the house can do—
An omelette made of the emu egg
    And a paddymelon stew.'

' 'Tis well, 'tis well,' said the bonny wee man;
    'I have eaten the wide world's meat,
But the food that is given wi' a right good will
    Is the sweetest food to eat.

'But the night draws on to the Christmas Day
    And I must rise and go,
For I have a mighty way to ride
    To the land of the Esquimaux.

'And it's there I must load my sledges up
    With the reindeers four-in-hand,
That go to the North, South, East, and West,
    To every Christian land.'

'To the Esquimaux,' said the dour good wife,
    'Ye suit my husband well!
For when he gets up on his journey horse
    He's a bit of a liar himsel'.'

Then out wi' a laugh went the bonny wee man
    To his old horse grazing nigh,
And away like a meteor flash they went
    Far off to the Northern sky.

When the children woke on the Christmas morn
    They chattered might and main—

Wi' a sword and gun for little son Jack,
   And a braw new doll for Jane,
And a packet o' nails for the twa emus;
   But the dour gude wife got nane.

'In re a Gentleman, One'

When an attorney is called before the Full Court to answer for any alleged misconduct it is not usual to publish his name until he is found guilty; until then the matter appears in the papers as, 'In re a Gentleman, One of the Attorneys of the Supreme Court,' or, more shortly, 'In re a Gentleman, One.'

We see it each day in the paper,
   And know that there's mischief in store;
That some unprofessional caper
   Has landed a shark on the shore.
We know there'll be plenty of trouble
   Before they get through with the fun,
Because he's been coming the double
   On clients, has 'Gentleman, One.'

Alas! for the gallant attorney,
   Intent upon cutting a dash,
Sets out on life's perilous journey
   With rather more cunning than cash.
And fortune at first is inviting—
   He struts his brief hour in the sun—
But, lo! on the wall is the writing
   Of Nemesis, 'Gentleman, One.'

For soon he runs short of the dollars,
   He fears he must go to the wall;
So Peter's trust-money he collars
   To pay off his creditor, Paul;
Then robs right and left—for he goes it
   In earnest when once he's begun.
Descensus averni—he knows it;
   It's easy for 'Gentleman, One.'

The crash comes as sure as the seasons;
    He loses his coin in a mine,
Or booming in land, or for reasons
    Connected with women and wine.
Or maybe the cards or the horses
    A share of the damage have done.
No matter; the end of the course is
    The same: '*Re* a Gentleman, One.'

He struggles a while to keep going,
    To stave off detection and shame;
But creditors clamorous growing
    Ere long put an end to the game.
At length the poor soldier of Satan
    His course to a finish has run—
And just think of Windeyer waiting
    To deal with 'a Gentleman, One!'

And some face it boldly, and brazen
    The shame and the utter disgrace;
While others, more sensitive, hasten
    Their names and their deeds to efface.
They snap the frail thread which the Furies
    And Fates have so cruelly spun.
May the Great Final Judge and His juries
    Have mercy on 'Gentleman, One!'

At the Melting of the Snow

There's a sunny southern land,
   And it's there that I would be
Where the big hills stand,
   In the South Countrie!
When the wattles bloom again,
   Then it's time for us to go
To the old Monaro country
   At the melting of the snow.

To the East or to the West,
   Or wherever you may be,
You will find no place
   Like the South Countrie.
For the skies are blue above,
   And the grass is green below,
In the old Monaro country
   At the melting of the snow.

Now the team is in the plough,
   And the thrushes start to sing,
And the pigeons on the bough
   Are rejoicing at the Spring.
So come my comrades all,
   Let us saddle up and go
To the old Monaro country
   At the melting of the snow.

Lay of the Motor Car

We're away! and the wind whistles shrewd
   In our whiskers and teeth;
And the granite-like grey of the road
   Seems to slide underneath.
As an eagle might sweep through the sky,
   So we sweep through the land;
And the pallid pedestrians fly
   When they hear us at hand.

We outpace, we outlast, we outstrip!
   Not the fast-fleeing hare,
Nor the racehorses under the whip,
   Nor the birds of the air
Can compete with our swiftness sublime,
   Our ease and our grace.
We annihilate chickens and time
   And policemen and space.

Do you mind that fat grocer who crossed?
   How he dropped down to pray
In the road when he saw he was lost;
   How he melted away
Underneath, and there rang through the fog
   His earsplitting squeal
As he went—Is that he or a dog,
   That stuff on the wheel?

When Dacey Rode the Mule

'Twas in a small, up-country town,
  When we were boys at school,
There came a circus with a clown
  And with a bucking mule.
The clown announced a scheme they had—
  The mule was such a king—
They'd give a crown to any lad
  Who'd ride him round the ring.
And, gentle reader, do not scoff
  Nor think the man a fool,
To buck a porous plaster off
  Was pastime to that mule.

The boys got on—he bucked like sin—
  He threw them in the dirt,
And then the clown would raise a grin
  By asking, 'Were they hurt?'
But Johnny Dacey came one night,
  The crack of all the school,
Said he, 'I'll win the crown all right,
  Bring in your bucking mule.'
The elephant went off his trunk
  The monkey played the fool
And all the band got blazing drunk
  When Dacey rode the mule.

But soon there rose an awful shout
  Of laughter, when the clown,
From somewhere in his pants drew out
  A little paper crown.
He placed the crown on Dacey's head,
  While Dacey looked a fool,
'Now, there's your crown, my lad,' he said,
  'For riding of the mule!'
The band struck up with 'Killaloe',
  And 'Rule Britannia, Rule',

And 'Young Man from the Country', too,
  When Dacey rode the mule.

Then Dacey, in a furious rage,
  For vengeance on the show
Ascended to the monkeys' cage
  And let the monkeys go;
The blue-tailed ape and chimpanzee
  He turned abroad to roam;
Good faith! It was a sight to see
  The people step for home.
For big baboons with canine snout
  Are spiteful, as a rule,
The people didn't sit it out
  When Dacey rode the mule.

And from the beasts that did escape
  The bushmen all declare
Were born some creatures partly ape
  And partly native bear.
They're rather few and far between;
  The race is nearly spent;
But some of them may still be seen
  In Sydney Parliament.
And when those legislators fight,
  And drink, and act the fool—
It all commenced that wretched night
  When Dacey rode the mule.

The Protest

I say 'e *isn't* Remorse!
   'Ow do I know?
Saw 'im on Riccarton course
   Two year ago!
Think I'd forget any 'orse?
   Course 'e's The Crow!

Bumper Maginnis and I,
   After a 'go',
Walkin' our 'orses to dry,
   I says, 'Hello!
What's that old black goin' by?'
   Bumper says, 'Oh!
That's an old caddy of Flanagan's
   —Runs as The Crow!'

Now they make out 'e's Remorse.
   Well, but I *know*.
Soon as I came on the course
   I says, ' 'Ello!
'Ere's the old Crow.'
Once a man's seen any 'orse,
   'Course 'e must know.
Sure as there's wood in this table,
   I say 'e's The Crow.

(Cross-examined by the Committee)

'Ow do I know the moke
   After one sight?
S'posin' you met a bloke
   Down town at night,
Wouldn't you know 'im again
    when you met 'im?
   That's *'im* all right!

What was the brand on 'is 'ide?
 I couldn't say.
Brands can be transmogrified.
 That ain't the way—
It's the *look* of a 'orse and the
  way that 'e moves
 That I'd know any day.

What was the boy on 'is back?
 Why, 'e went past
All of a minute, and off down the track.
 —'The 'orse went as fast?'
True, so 'e did! But, my eyes, what a treat!
 'Ow can I notice the 'ands and the seat
Of each bumble-faced kid of a boy that I meet?
 Lor'! What a question to ast!

(Protest dismissed)

Reconstruction

From a Farmer's Point of View

So, the bank has bust its boiler! And in six or seven year
   It will pay me all my money back—of course!
But the horse will perish waiting while the grass is
      germinating,
   And I reckon I'll be something like the horse.

There's the ploughing to be finished and the ploughmen
      want their pay,
   And I'd like to wire the fence and sink a tank;
But I own I'm fairly beat how I'm going to make ends meet
   With my money in a reconstructed bank.

'It's a safe and sure investment!' But it's one I can't afford,
   For I've got to meet my bills and pay the rent,
And the cash I had provided (so these meetings have
      decided)
   Shall be collared by the bank at three per cent.

I can draw out half my money, so they tell me, from the
      Crown;
   But—it's just enough to drive a fellow daft—
My landlord's quite distressed, by this very bank he's
      pressed,
   And he'll sell me up, to pay his overdraft.

There's my nearest neighbour, Johnson, owed this self-same
      bank a debt,
   Every feather off his poor old back they pluck't,
For they set to work to shove him, and they sold his house
      above him,
   Lord! They never gave *him* time to reconstuct.

And their profits from the business have been twenty-five
    per cent,
  Which, I reckon, is a pretty tidy whack,
And I think it's only proper, now the thing has come a
    cropper,
  That they ought to pay a little of it back.

I have read about 'reserve funds', 'banking freeholds', and
    the like,
  Till I thought the bank had thousands of as*sets*,
And it strikes me very funny that they take a fellow's money
  When they haven't got enough to pay their debts.

And they say they've lent my money, and they can't get
    paid it back.
  I know their rates per cent were tens and twelves;
And if now they've made a blunder after scooping all this
    plunder,
  Why, they ought to fork the money out themselves.

So all you bank shareholders, if you won't pay what you
    owe,
  You will find that on your bank will fall a blight;
And the reason is because it's simply certain that deposits
  Will be stopped, the bank will bust, and serve you right!

The Ghost of the Murderer's Hut

My horse had been lamed in the foot
   In the rocks at the back of the run,
So I camped at the Murderer's Hut,
   At the place where the murder was done.

The walls were all spattered with gore,
   A terrible symbol of guilt;
And the bloodstains were fresh on the floor
   Where the blood of the victim was spilt.

The wind hurried past with a shout,
   The thunderstorm doubled its din
As I shrank from the danger without,
   And recoiled from the horror within.

When lo! at the window a shape,
   A creature of infinite dread;
A thing with the face of an ape,
   And with eyes like the eyes of the dead.

With the horns of a fiend, and a skin
   That was hairy as satyr or elf,
And a long, pointed beard on its chin—
   My God! 'twas the Devil himself.

In anguish I sank on the floor,
   With terror my features were stiff,
Till *the thing* gave a kind of a roar,
   Ending up with a resonant 'Biff!'

Then a cheer burst aloud from my throat,
   For the thing that my spirit did vex
Was naught but an elderly goat—
   Just a goat of the masculine sex.

When his master was killed he had fled,
    And now, by the dingoes bereft,
The nannies were all of them dead,
    And only the billy was left.

So we had him brought in on a stage
    To the house where, in style, he can strut,
And he lives to a fragrant old age
    As the Ghost of the Murderer's Hut.

The Federal Bus Conductor and the Old Lady

Now 'urry, Mrs New South Wales, and come along of us,
We're all a-goin' ridin' in the Federation 'bus.
A fam'ly party, don't you know—yes, Queensland's comin',
    too.
You can't afford it! Go along! We've kep' box seat for you.
The very one of all the lot that can afford it best,
You'll only have to pay your share the same as all the rest.

You say your sons is workin' men, and can't afford to ride!
Well, *all* our sons is workin' men, a-smokin' up outside.
You think you might be drove to smash by some unskilful
    bloke!
Well, aint't we all got necks ourselves? And we don't want
    'em broke.
You bet your life we're not such fools but what we'll do our
    best
To keep from harm—for harm to one is harm to all the rest.

Now, don't go trudgin' on alone, but get aboard the trap;
That basket, labelled 'Capital', you take it in your lap!
It's nearly time we made a start, so let's 'ave no more talk:
You 'urry up and get aboard, or else stop out and walk.
We've got a flag; we've got a band; our 'orses travels fast;
Ho! Right away, Bill! Let 'em go! The old 'un's come at last!

The Lost Leichhardt

An English scientific society is fitting out a
pioneering party to search for traces of the lost
explorer Leichhardt

Another search for Leichhardt's tomb,
  Though fifty years have fled
Since Leichhardt vanished in the gloom,
  Our one Illustrious Dead!

But daring men from Britain's shore,
  The fearless bulldog breed,
Renew the fearful task once more,
  Determined to succeed.

Rash men, that know not what they seek,
  Will find their courage tried.
For things have changed on Cooper's Creek
  Since Ludwig Leichhardt died.

Along where Leichhardt journeyed slow
  And toiled and starved in vain;
These rash excursionists must go
  Per Queensland railway train.

Out on those deserts lone and drear
  The fierce Australian black
Will say—'You show it pint o' beer,
  It show you Leichhardt track!'

And loud from every squatter's door
  Each pioneering swell
Will hear the wild pianos roar
  The strains of 'Daisy Bell'.

The watchers in those forests vast
  Will see, at fall of night,

137

Commercial travellers bounding past
  And darting out of sight.

About their path a fearful fate
  Will hover always near.
A dreadful scourge that lies in wait—
  The Longreach Horehound Beer!

And then, to crown this tale of guilt,
  They'll find some scurvy knave,
Regardless of their quest, has built
  A pub on Leichhardt's grave!

Ah, yes! Those British pioneers
  Had best at home abide,
For things have changed in fifty years
  Since Ludwig Leichhardt died.

Now Listen to Me and I'll Tell You My Views

Now listen to me and I'll tell you my views concerning the
    African war,
And the man who upholds any different views, the same is a
    rotten Pro-Boer!
(Though I'm getting a little bit doubtful myself, as it drags
    on week after week:
But it's better not ask any questions at all—let us silence all
    doubts with a shriek!)

And first let us shriek the unstinted abuse that the Tory
    Press prefer—De Wet is a madman, and Steyn is a liar,
    and Kruger a pitiful cur!
(Though I think if Oom Paul—as old as he is—were to walk
    down the Strand with his gun,
A lot of these heroes would hide in the sewers or take to
    their heels and run!
For Paul he has fought like a man in his day, but now that
    he's feeble and weak
And tired, and lonely, and old and grey, of course it's quite
    safe to shriek!)

And next let us join in the bloodthirsty shriek, Hooray for
    Lord Kitchener's 'bag'!
For the fireman's torch and the hangman's cord—they are
    hung on the English Flag!
In the front of our brave old army! Whoop! the farmhouse
    blazes bright.
And their women weep and their children die—how dare
    they presume to fight!
For none of them dress in a uniform, the same as by rights
    they ought.
They're fighting in rags and in naked feet, like Wallace's
    Scotchmen fought!

(And they clothe themselves from our captured troops—and
    they're catching them every week;
And they don't hang *them*—and the shame is ours, but we
    cover the shame with a shriek!)

And, lastly, we'll shriek the political shriek as we sit in the
    dark and doubt;
Where the Birmingham Judas led us in, and there's no one
    to lead us out.
And Rosebery—whom we depended upon!
    Would only the Oracle speak!
'You go to the Grocers,' says he, 'for your laws!'
    By heavens! it's time to shriek!

Australia Today—1916

They came from the lower levels
   Deep down in the Brilliant mine;
From the wastes where the whirlwind revels,
   Whirling the leaves of pine.

On the Western plains, where the Darling flows,
   And the dust storms wheel and shift,
The teamster loosened his yokes and bows,
   And turned his team adrift.

On the Western stations, far and wide,
   There's many an empty pen,
For the 'ringers' have cast the machines aside
   And answered the call for men.

On the lucerne flats where the stream runs slow,
   And the Hunter finds the sea,
The women are driving the mowers now,
   With the children at their knee.

For the men have gone, as a man must go,
   At the call of the rolling drums;
For the men have sworn that the Turks shall know
   When the old battalion comes.

Column of companies by the right,
   Steady in strong array,
With the sun on the bayonets gleaming bright,
   The battalion marched away.

They battled, the old battalion,
   Through the toil of the training camps,
Sweated and strove at lectures,
   By the light of the stinking lamps.

Marching, shooting, and drilling;
    Steady and slow and stern;
Awkward and strange, but willing
    All of their jobs to learn.

Learning to use the rifle;
    Learning to use the spade;
Deeming fatigue a trifle
    During each long parade.

Till at last they welded
    Into a concrete whole,
And there grew in the old battalion
    A kind of battalion's soul.

Brotherhood never was like it;
    Friendship is not the word;
But deep in that body of marching men
    The soul of a nation stirred.

And like one man with a single thought
    Cheery and confident;
Ready for all that the future brought,
    The old battalion went.

Column of companies by the right,
    Steady in strong array,
With the sun on the bayonets gleaming bright,
    The battalion marched away.

How shall we tell of their landing
    By the hills where the foe were spread,
And the track of the old battalion
    Was marked by the Turkish dead?

With the dash that discipline teaches,
    Though the hail of the shrapnel flew,
And the forts were raking the beaches,
    And the toll of the dead men grew.

They fixed their grip on the gaunt hillside
 With a pluck that has won them fame;
And the home-folks know that the dead men died
 For the pride of Australia's name.

Column of companies by the right,
 To the beat of the rolling drums;
With honours gained in a stirring fight
 The old Battalion comes!

The Army Mules

Oh the airman's game is a showman's game for we all of us
   watch him go
With his roaring soaring aeroplane and his bombs for the
   blokes below,
Over the railways and over the dumps, over the Hun and
   the Turk,
You'll hear him mutter, 'What ho, she bumps,' when the
   Archies get to work.
But not of him is the song I sing, though he follow the
   eagle's flight,
And with shrapnel holes in his splintered wing comes home
   to his roost at night.
He may silver his wings on the shining stars, he may look
   from the throne on high,
He may follow the flight of the wheeling kite in the blue
   Egyptian sky,
But he's only a hero built to plan, turned out by the Army
   schools,
And I sing of the rankless, thankless man who hustles the
   Army mules.

Now where he comes from and where he lives is a mystery
   dark and dim,
And it's rarely indeed that the General gives a D.S.O. to him.
The stolid infantry digs its way like a mole in a ruined wall;
The cavalry lends a tone, they say, to what were else but a
   brawl;
The Brigadier of the Mounted Fut like a cavalry Colonel
   swanks
When he goeth abroad like a gilded nut to receive the
   General's thanks;
The Ordnance man is a son of a gun and his lists are a
   standing joke;
You order, 'Choke arti Jerusalem one' for Jerusalem
   artichoke.

The Medicals shine with a number nine, and the men of the
    great R.E.,
Their Colonels are Methodists, married or mad, and some of
    them all the three;
In all these units the road to fame is taught in the Army
    schools,
But a man has got to be born to the game when he tackles
    the Army mules.

For if you go where the depots are as the dawn is breaking
    grey,
By the waning light of the morning star as the dust cloud
    clears away,
You'll see a vision among the dust like a man and a mule
    combined—
It's the kind of thing you must take on trust for its outlines
    aren't defined,
A thing that whirls like a spinning top and props like a
    three-legged stool,
And you find it's a long-legged Queensland boy convincing
    an Army mule.
And the rider sticks to the hybrid's hide like paper sticks to
    a wall,
For a 'magnoon' Waler is next to ride with every chance of a
    fall,
It's a rough-house game and a thankless game, and it isn't a
    game for a fool,
For an army's fate and a nation's fame may turn on an Army
    mule.

And if you go to the front-line camp where the sleepless
    outposts lie,
At the dead of night you can hear the tramp of the mule
    train toiling by.
The rattle and clink of a leading-chain, the creak of the
    lurching load,
As the patient, plodding creatures strain at their task in the
    shell-torn road,

Through the dark and the dust you may watch them go till
the dawn is grey in the sky,
And only the watchful pickets know when the 'All-night
Corps' goes by.
And far away as the silence falls when the last of the train
has gone,
A weary voice through the darkness calls: 'Get on there,
men, get on!'
It isn't a hero, built to plan, turned out by the modern
schools,
It's only the Army Service man a-driving his Army mules.

Australian Scenery

The Mountains

A land of sombre, silent hills, where mountain cattle go
By twisted tracks, on sidelings steep, where giant gum trees
grow
And the wind replies, in the river oaks, to the song of the
stream below.

A land where the hills keep watch and ward, silent and
wide awake
As those who sit by a dead campfire, and wait for the dawn
to break,
Or those who watched by the Holy Cross for the dead
Redeemer's sake.

A land where silence lies so deep that sound itself is dead
And a gaunt grey bird, like a homeless soul, drifts, noiseless,
overhead
And the world's great story is left untold, and the message
is left unsaid.

The Plains

A land, as far as the eye can see, where the waving grasses
grow
Or the plains are blackened and burnt and bare, where the
false mirages go
Like shifting symbols of hope deferred—land where you
never know.

Land of plenty or land of want, where the grey Companions
dance,
Feast or famine, or hope or fear, and in all things land of
chance,
Where Nature pampers or Nature slays, in her ruthless, red,
romance.

And we catch a sound of a fairy's song, as the wind goes
 whipping by,
Or a scent like incense drifts along from the herbage ripe
 and dry
—Or the dust storms dance on their ballroom floor, where
 the bones of the cattle lie.

A Dog's Mistake

In Doggerel Verse

He had drifted in among us as a straw drifts with the tide,
He was just a wand'ring mongrel from the weary world
　　outside;
He was not aristocratic, being mostly ribs and hair,
With a hint of spaniel parents and a touch of native bear.

He was very poor and humble and content with what he
　　got,
So we fed him bones and biscuits, till he heartened up a lot;
Then he growled and grew aggressive, treating orders with
　　disdain,
Till at last he bit the butcher, which would argue want of
　　brain.

Now the butcher, noble fellow, was a sport beyond belief,
And instead of bringing actions he brought half a shin of
　　beef,
Which he handed on to Fido, who received it as a right
And removed it to the garden, where he buried it at night.

'Twas the means of his undoing, for my wife, who'd stood
　　his friend,
To adopt a slang expression, 'went in off the deepest end',
For among the pinks and pansies, the gloxinias and the
　　gorse
He had made an excavation like a graveyard for a horse.

Then we held a consultation which decided on his fate:
'Twas in anger more than sorrow that we led him to the
　　gate,
And we handed him the beef-bone as provision for the day,
Then we opened wide the portal and we told him, 'On your
　　way.'

The Billy-Goat Overland

Come all ye lads of the droving days, ye gentlemen
　　unafraid,
I'll tell you all of the greatest trip that ever a drover made,
For we rolled our swags, and we packed our bags, and
　　taking our lives in hand,
We started away with a thousand goats, on the billy-goat
　　overland.

There wasn't a fence that'd hold the mob, or keep 'em from
　　their desires;
They skipped along the top of the posts and cake-walked on
　　the wires.
And where the lanes had been stripped of grass and the
　　paddocks were nice and green,
The goats they travelled outside the lanes and we rode in
　　between.

The squatters started to drive them back, but that was no
　　good at all,
Their horses ran for the lick of their lives from the scent that
　　was like a wall:
And never a dog had pluck or gall in front of the mob to
　　stand
And face the charge of a thousand goats on the billy-goat
　　overland.

We found we were hundreds over strength when we
　　counted out the mob;
And they put us in jail for a crowd of thieves that travelled
　　to steal and rob:
For every goat between here and Bourke, when he scented
　　our spicy band,
Had left his home and his work to join in the billy-goat
　　overland.

Black Harry's Team

No soft-skinned Durham steers are they,
   No Devons plump and red,
But brindled, black, and iron-grey
   That mark the mountain-bred;
For mountain-bred and mountain-broke,
   With sullen eyes agleam,
No stranger's hand could put a yoke
   On old Black Harry's team.

Pull out, pull out, at break of morn
   The creeks are running white,
And Tiger, Spot, and Snailey-horn
   Must bend their bows by night;
And axles, wheels and flooring boards
   Are swept with flying spray
As, shoulder-deep, through mountain fords
   The leaders feel their way.

He needs no sign of cross or kirn
   To guide him as he goes,
For every twist and every turn
   That old black leader knows.
Up mountains steep they heave and strain
   Where never wheel has rolled,
And what the toiling leaders gain
   The body bullocks hold.

Where eaglehawks their eyries make,
   On sidelings steep and blind,
He rigs the good old-fashioned brake—
   A tree tied on behind.
Up mountains, straining to the full,
   Each poler plays his part—
The sullen, stubborn, bullock pull
   That breaks a horse's heart.

Beyond the furthest bridle track
    His wheels have blazed the way;
The forest giants, burnt and black,
    Are earmarked by his dray.
Through belts of scrub where messmates grow
    His juggernaut has rolled,
For stumps and saplings have to go
    When Harry's team takes hold.

On easy grade and rubber tyre
    The tourist car goes through;
They halt a moment to admire
    The far-flung mountain view.
The tourist folk would be amazed
    If they could get to know
They take the track Black Harry blazed
    A hundred years ago.

Buffalo Country

Out where the grey streams glide,
Sullen and deep and slow,
And the alligators slide
From the mud to the depths below
Or drift on the stream like a floating death,
Where the fever comes on the south wind's breath,
There is the buffalo.

Out on the big lagoons,
Where the Regia lilies float,
And the Nankin heron croons
With a deep ill-omened note,
In the ooze and the mud of the swamps below
Lazily wallows the buffalo,
Buried to nose and throat.

From the hunter's gun he hides
In the jungles dark and damp,
Where the slinking dingo glides
And the flying foxes camp;
Hanging like myriad fiends in line
Where the trailing creepers twist and twine
And the sun is a sluggish lamp.

On the edge of the rolling plains
Where the coarse cane grasses swell,
Lush with the tropic rains
In the noontide's drowsy spell,
Slowly the buffalo grazes through
Where the brolgas dance, and the jabiru
Stands like a sentinel.

All that the world can know
Of the wild and the weird is here,
Where the black men come and go
With their boomerang and spear,

And the wild duck darken the evening sky
As they fly to their nests in the reed beds high
When the tropic night is near.

Queensland Mounted Infantry

There's a very well-built fellow, with a swinging sort of
    stride,
  About as handy sort as I have seen.
A rough and tumble fellow that is born to fight and ride
  And he's over here a-fighting for the Queen.

He's Queensland Mounted Infantry—compounded 'orse
    and foot.
  He'll climb a cliff or gallop down a flat.
He's cavalry to travel but he's infantry to shoot.
  And you'll know him by the feathers in his hat!

Campin' Round Coonamble

Written when reporting for the Sydney Morning Herald *on the shearing troubles at Coonamble.*

Campin' round Coonamble,
   Keepin' up the strike,
Through the black soil country
   Plugging on the 'bike';
Half a thousand shearers,
   What had we to gain
Campin' round Coonamble,
   Campin' in the rain?

Twenty bob a hundred
   Shearing with machines!
Good enough in these times
   We know what it means—
Sinking tanks and fencing,
   Shearing's better pay
Twenty bob a hundred
   Twenty bob a day!

Every little farmer
   Up Monaro side
Sends the boys a-shearing,
   Hoping to provide
Something for the homestead;
   All his hopes are vain,
While we're round Coonamble,
   Campin' in the rain.

Up at old man Tobin's
   First pen on the right,
Don't I know his wethers,
   Know 'em all by sight!

Many a year I shore 'em
  Like to shear again,
Better game than campin'
  Campin' in the rain.

What's the use of talking
  Five-and-twenty bob,
While there's hundreds hungry
  Looking for a job?
Darling Harbour casuals,
  Hollow in the cheek,
Cadging from the Government
  Two days' work a week.

When with peal of trumpets,
  And with beat of drums,
Labour's great millennium
  Actually comes;
When each white Australian,
  Master of his craft,
Keeps a foreign servant
  Just to do the graft;

When the price of shearing
  Goes to fifty bob,
And there's no man hungry
  Looking for a job;
Then, if they oppress us,
  Then we'll go again
Campin' round Coonamble,
Campin' in the rain.

INDEX OF FIRST LINES